HAPP!NESS MADE EASY

MICAEL DAHLEN

HAPP!NESS MADE EASY

THE SCIENCE-BASED STEPS TO FEEL JUST A BIT BETTER

A LITTLE BOOK ABOUT A BIG QUESTION

✳ Volante

Happiness Made Easy : The Science-based
Steps to Feel Just a Bit Better
© Micael Dahlen & Volante 2022

Volante
Stora Nygatan 7
111 27 Stockholm
www.volante.se

Original title: En liten bok om lycka
Translation: Elizabeth DeNoma
Cover and inlay: Miroslav Sokcic
ISBN: 978-91-7965-385-9

CONTENT

WHAT CAN HAPPINESS RESEARCH TEACH US?

How happy are you?

THE QUESTION obviously needs asking in a book about happiness, so let's deal with it right away. Think about how you're feeling for a moment. On a scale from 1 to 10, where would place yourself just now? Circle a number:

1 2 3 4 5 6 7 8 9 10

My guess is that you put yourself in the upper half. Otherwise, you probably wouldn't be reading this book right now. Who could bring themselves to read a book at all, let alone one about happiness, if they were feeling miserable? Everyone slips down on the scale for one reason or another at some point, but most of us will likely find ourselves on the upper half of it much of the time (and there are a bunch of studies showing that very thing, some of which I've been involved in).

I'm guessing, though, you didn't circle 10 either, because who'd feel the need to read a book about happiness—who even has the time and the wherewithal to consider it—if they're experiencing maximum happiness? If I'm wrong, and at this moment you happen to find yourself at a 10 on the happiness scale, you should immediately put this book down and go savor it. Enjoy yourself to the fullest and let that wonderful peak level of happiness rub off on as many people around you as possible.

Enjoy it while it lasts.

Most of us reach the high end of the happiness scale from time to time, but it doesn't happen that often and it doesn't last that long. These occasions are usually easy to recall, and at the very most they last 3 months. The great romance, the great success, the great change in your life—the kind of thing that you can put "the great" in front of. That's just what it's like, and I know because I've asked lots of people around the world—by now probably around 100,000. I've asked these people to circle their happiness level *right now*, or *on the whole* (it doesn't really make much difference: life in general is made up of a lot of *right nows*, which are only occasionally unusually low or high); almost everyone places themselves on the upper part of the scale, but not at 10.

Does the question "How happy are you?" capture the whole truth? Surely happiness is something more—something much more—than answering a question. It's something that can be felt in your heart, in your whole body. Something that makes you feel good, calm, exhilarated, full of life. Right?

Yeah, sure. Happiness expresses itself through your heart rate and blood pressure. Cortisol levels and brain waves. Hormones and neurotransmitters such as dopamine, serotonin, testosterone and adrenaline. Even our resistance to colds. There are studies about all of that. That's fantastic, isn't it?

All of those chemicals, which affect your mood, your performance, how you think, and how good you feel, have been shown to be linked to happiness. The same applies to your ability to be creative, which is something I myself discovered in a study. And other researchers have established that it also applies to being lucky in love (which turns out not to be just about luck), success in sports, school, career, and even in court(!). Happier people do, on average, get a bit more of all of that.

You'll live longer, too. Happiness has been shown to have roughly as much influence on how long you live as smoking does, but working in opposite directions, of course. If you're a really happy smoker then it should even out. If you are a happy nonsmoker, then you can look forward to a long life. And if you are an unhappy smoker then you should hurry up and read this book while there's still time.

So, it's hardly surprising that the question is worth asking: How happy are you? And yes, it's enough to ask that sole question instead of measuring all those different things in your body, because they're linked, and that's why the question gets asked in almost all research on happiness. It can be phrased in different ways: How happy are you? How satisfied are you with life? How good do you feel? But the answers are usually the same.

This kind of a question doesn't provide a complete and perfect answer, but it does give a sufficiently good picture and it's simple enough to ask anybody in any context, even somebody who at this moment is busy reading a little book about happiness.

In the rest of the book, we'll look in more detail at why you circled that particular number on the scale, and how you can wind up a bit higher. I won't promise that you will end up at the top of the scale; I'm more likely to promise that you won't be able to lodge yourself at the top for the long term. That would be abnormal.

Research on happiness actually has its starting point in the fact that happiness is indeed abnormal, literally: the first research article about happiness was published in the tellingly named *Journal of Abnormal Psychology* just over 100 years ago, in 1917. Titled "Eupathics – A program for mental hygiene," the article was written by Abraham Myerson, psychiatrist and neurosurgeon best known for having given his name to a method for detecting early-stage Parkinson's by repetitively tapping between eyebrows (if this makes you start blinking uncontrollably, then it would be best to put the book down and inform a doctor that you have Myerson's sign).

If you were to ask Freud—and that would be fun, wouldn't it, if it were possible?—he would probably answer that it's perverse to be completely happy. A few years after Myerson's article, in 1929, Freud wrote a book about how happiness means always following your most primitive desires—often sexual and rather weird (think British members of Parliament and oranges). These desires are regarded as perverse in a civilized society, said Freud, who placed blame for the human inability to be happy upon civilization and gave us the book titled *Das Unbehagen in der Kultur (Civilization and Its Discontents)*.

If you ask me, the answer instead is that the idea of sitting at the top of the happiness scale leads to *happychondria*. It convinces us into thinking that we are unhappier than we are because we think that we should be happier than we are, that we should always be at the top of the scale. Which is precisely why I asked you "How happy are you?" and not "Are you happy?". Because happiness stretches right across the range, and instead of worrying and becoming unhappy about not being able to stay at the top end of the scale (many of us can't even get there for short visits, but we'll come back to that), we ought to appreciate how happy we actually are—wherever we find ourselves on the scale. And dare to hope that we'll get a bit happier.

That is what those links look like, too, between being a bit happier and being a little less inclined to catch a cold, or being creative, or "lucky" in court (now, I hope that you will never find yourself in a court of law, but I love that particular correlation). It's not about happy people in comparison to the rest of us unhappy happychondriacs, but that *a little more* of one thing (happiness, regardless of where you fall on the scale) is interconnected with a little more of another (such as honesty in filing your taxes, to take another example that I found in a study, which is fitting here because this reduces the likelihood that you will need to rely on luck in court).

As we will see, the links can go in both directions. Just like you become a bit more creative when you are a bit happier, you can also become a bit happier *from* being a bit more creative, to use an example that we'll return to. Or you will become both a bit healthier when you are a bit happier and a bit happier from being healthier. It can be enough to shake off a cold. I carried out a study of 1,000 Swedes and found that those who had recently recovered from a cold were significantly happier than average.

So. Now let's get going with some advice. What can happiness research tell us about how to become a little bit happier (and a little less of a happychondriac)?*

1

CHOOSE YOUR PARENTS CAREFULLY (YES, IT CAN BE DONE)

HOW HAPPY you are depends to a great degree on chance. That's why in my native Swedish the word for "happy" and "luck" are the same: *lycka*. We took the word from the German *Glück*, a word from the 12th century which then meant "chance" or "coincidence." The same applies with the English "happiness," which originally comes from *hap*, a similarly ancient word for chance/coincidence.

It is not entirely clear why the Germans and the English came to the conclusion that chance was the best way to describe happiness, but I would guess that it was because they didn't find any other explanation for why some people were more satisfied with life and more subjectively well-off than others, regardless of what happened or what they did in life (they probably didn't use those particular terms in the Middle Ages, research into happiness not starting, as we know, until 1917). According to this view, people simply happened to be born with a bit more or a bit less happiness, completely by chance.

Nowadays, we know how right they were. Everyone is born

with a lottery ticket. About 50% of how happy you are depends on which genes you were born with. Happiness researchers have come to that conclusion by measuring happiness in monozygotic (i.e., identical) twins, who have identical genes. Researchers have asked all manner of twins how happy they are. Children, adults, teenagers, pensioners. Swedish, German, American, Canadian, Kenyan, Chinese. Even 128 Scottish chimpanzees (they found it hard to understand the question, so independent observers were tasked with circling a number based on their impressions). In all, there is data on almost 6,000 twins that show that however different the lives they lead—they may have been separated at birth and never have met, moved to opposite sides of the Earth, had completely different family situations and careers (this doesn't apply to the chimpanzees)—their happiness in every given situation corresponds to nearly 40% on average. In measurements of their "base happiness"—how you feel when you wake up in the morning before anything at all has happened in your day and you're hardly awake enough to know your own name—the correlation is close to 80%. And if we combine those measurements, we end up at approximately 50%.

Researchers don't entirely agree on exactly which genes are involved. Some contend that the major happiness gene is 5-HTT, which governs the transport of serotonin. Others are of the opinion that it is a gene with the not entirely catchy name FAAH rs324420, which governs our endurance for stress and pain. Perhaps it's both of them and even a few more that haven't yet been discovered. What we do know, in any case, is that you get the variant you're going to have of whichever genes they happen to be when you are born, whether you want them or not, and you are stuck with them for the rest of your life.

Which means that your happiness is your very own (and half of your twin's, if you happen to have one).

Your happiness is unique. Nobody can be happy in exactly the same way and on exactly the same level as you. This means that you can't actually compare your happiness with that of others; you can't have other people as your measure. If, for example, you find it easier than others to be happy, then enjoy it, but don't fret if you don't. This doesn't mean that you're unhappy; it simply means that your happiness is on another level and functions in another way.

I have to remind myself of this, and I tattooed a flower on my right hand to not forget. As far back as I can remember, I have been envious of people who find it easy to laugh, who start the day with a smile on their lips. I wished that I too could be one of those people who see everything in positive terms. I've been ashamed because I'm bad at being carefree or bubbly, thinking there must be something wrong with me. Now I look at my flower tattoo instead and think about how it blossoms by finding the sun regardless of where it has roots. That helps a little.

But as the title of this chapter makes clear, I have another tip:

Choose your parents carefully.

Unfortunately, it's not that easy to choose your biological parents. It is, however, a good tip for those of you who want to have happy children: choose a happy partner. This applies especially to the father, who according to the genetic researchers has a few more expressive genes—60/40 is the rough estimate of the balance. Or at least try to make sure your partner is as happy as possible during the time you "produce" your child (a Spanish research team last year published an article which argued that the parents' mood is transmitted into their eggs and sperm).

But this isn't just about biology. Those of us who have been gifted families with stepchildren and stepparents in various combinations know this, and so do LGBTQA families. As do the researchers who studied the happiness of more than 3,000 Germans over a period of 25 years, from adolescence to middle age, and compared it with their parents' happiness. As long as they stayed in touch, the parents continued to influence their children's happiness, by their own happiness (especially the mothers') "infecting" their children, by their community, and by their behavior which the children mimicked and used as a model. The researchers' summarized that the parents affected as much as 25% of the children's happiness through family ties. Pretty amazing.

And even more amazing is that, unlike your genes, you can actually choose your family ties—who you want to share your community and happiness with and who you want to use as a model.

Call them mentors if you like, or what about a Super Mom? The word for mother originally meant something like "a person who provides nourishment," somebody who gives you the energy to grow. Or do as they do in Okinawa, Japan, and become parents to each other. They call it *moai*: a group of friends who take turns supporting each other through life, giving advice and emotional assistance if somebody becomes ill or even if they have money problems. Even though years can pass between moments of support, researchers are of the opinion that the security of knowing that there is somebody who you can contact at any time at all and who will help you when necessary helps explain why people in Okinawa historically have had the highest life expectancy in the world.

Our biological inheritance thus determines our happiness level a bit more that it is perhaps comfortable to admit. But the rest of this book is about a lot more that can still be influenced—in lots of different ways, believe it or not.

And the next chapter is actually about that very thing: believing.

»PARENTS INFLUENCE UP TO AN
ENTIRE 25% OF YOUR HAPPINESS
THROUGH FAMILY TIES.«

2
BELiEVE

BELIEVING IN something is a sort of "happy pill." Literally. Researchers at Karolinska Institute in Stockholm found that out when they showed people unpleasant news photos and measured their anxiety. The ones who were given happy pills before seeing the photos experienced less anxiety than the ones who hadn't. When the researchers later carried out the same experiment, but instead used sugar-coated pills which they claimed were happy pills, the effects were the same. The people who thought they had been given happy pills experienced a lot less anxiety than those who didn't get any pills. When the researchers scanned the pill takers' brains, the images of those who took happy pills looked more or less identical to those who only believed they had taken happy pills.

You will surely have heard about similar effects, when people perform or feel better because they believe they have been given a miracle medicine, even though they haven't. This is called a placebo, which comes from a medieval Latin word whose approximate original meaning was "I shall please God." As early as the Middle Ages, they seem to have linked religion with some sort of well-being (which at that time wasn't yet what we would call happiness, an idea that didn't make its breakthrough until much later).

Since then, study after study after study have shown that religion has a positive effect on how happy people are. Eight-year-olds who believe in God are a bit happier. College students who believe in God are a bit happier. Retirees. Hungarians. The interesting thing with the Hungarians is not just that they are Hungarians, but that the researchers carried out comprehensive studies on them before and after the fall of the Iron Curtain and could ascertain that those people who believed in God were not affected as much, while the rest of the population were a lot less satisfied with life when the entire system and economy collapsed.

Longitudinal studies, which follow the same people over a long period, show that those who during their lifetime join a religion climb a little bit higher up on the happiness scale and stay there, while people who leave a religion take a little step downwards. Forty thousand Muslims in 32 different countries experience an increase in happiness during Ramadan, despite life having become harder, in the form of hunger and diminished economic productivity (small surprise that the study was conducted by economics professors) because religion during that particular month becomes a bit more apparent in everyday life. The same pattern applies for Jews on the Sabbath.

Does it make any difference which religion you belong to? Yes, but only if you are between 10 and 12 years of age, and only a teeny bit. When researchers compared 38,000 10- to 12-year-olds in 16 countries, they found that Christians, Muslims, and Jews were just as happy, while Buddhists and Hindus were a tiny bit less happy. One explanation could be that Buddhism and Hinduism don't have as simple and clear routines and symbols, which make it easier for children to have faith. That could also explain why the small difference in happiness between the religions disappears when we examine people in adulthood.

It doesn't really matter which faith you have. You don't even need to believe in God. You can have faith in science, for example. When Iranian researchers compared belief in a God and belief in science among university students, they found that these influenced happiness in exactly the same way.

But what about aliens? you might ask. (At least I hope you ask, because I really want to tell you about them. And if you hadn't thought about it before, at least you must be curious now, right?) And yes, there is research about that, too. An American team of researchers has carried out a series of studies on the theme, and one of their findings was that people who believe that we are going to encounter alien life in the future are a bit more positive on average. The same applies to people who read the news about Allan Hills 84001, a Martian meteorite first discovered in the Alan Hills in Antarctica in 1984 and later found to contain microorganisms seen by some as evidence of extraterrestrial life.

I wish I thought of doing that study myself. But I did do

another fun one—on vegans. It still seems to be slightly unclear if eating vegan food makes you happier or not (and as a vegan myself, I'd really like to know). On the one hand, an epidemiological study of 10,000 Brits showed that those who only ate a vegan diet were almost twice as likely to suffer from depression. On the other hand, an experiment was carried out in Arizona which showed that meat eaters who had to switch to a meat-free diet jumped up a little bit on the scale when the researchers measured their happiness after 2 weeks. So, I carried out a study which might explain how the results could differ. When I asked 2,000 Swedes how happy they were, and then asked what sort of food they ate, it turned out that the vegans sat just under the average.

I can only speculate as to why. Perhaps it is because of an iron deficiency, or perhaps because the selection of vegan food available is still a little more limited. Or maybe they're more worried about the climate and the animals that other people are consuming? But when I asked people what sort of food they ate *first* and *then* measured their happiness, the vegans (who had now reminded themselves that they were vegans) lay well above average. Their belief in their diet made vegans happier than everybody else.

So, my advice is to believe. In God, in science, in aliens, in your diet, or your exercise routine. The research on happiness and religion shows several happiness advantages that you can totally benefit from regardless of what it is that you believe in.

A belief, a faith, gives you an identity: a Muslim, a vegan, or simply an American in the Midwest who swears that he/she was abducted by aliens and subjected to experiments before being dumped in a field. It gives you a pleasant feeling of security and maybe even outright pride.

It also gives you a sense of community with others who believe, exercise, or eat in the same way as you, and with whom you can talk, share experiences, and create a community. That explains why the number of times Christians go to church is positively correlated with their happiness.

Faith can even give you advantages if you believe in something that nobody else believes in (for example, that your dog Sam can talk and possesses the collected wisdom of the entire universe). It gives you meaning and turns your life into something more than just a sequence of weekdays repeated 52 times a year. A massive study of almost 100,000 people in 94 countries showed that people with faith experienced a stronger sense of purpose, which made them happier, regardless of what happens.

Faith doesn't just give greater meaning to your life and a sense of purpose to the passing days (which isn't really "just"). I found a study which shows that it also gives retirees a stronger feeling that they are needed and valuable, and I am pretty sure that the same applies to all of us, regardless of whether we are 8 or 80.

You can even become happier from believing that the end of the world is close (yes, there's a study about even that). But that is not something I would recommend (I will, however, admit that it makes me a little bit happier when I think that this book could be called *The End of the World is Close: A Little Book About Happiness*).

»IT DOESN'T REALLY MAKE ANY DIFFERENCE WHICH FAITH YOU HAVE. WHEN RESEARCHERS COMPARED FAITH IN GOD AND FAITH IN SCIENCE AMONG UNIVERSITY STUDENTS, THEY FOUND BOTH INFLUENCED HAPPINESS IN EXACTLY THE SAME WAY.«

3

CLAIM VICTORY IN ADVANCE

STUDIES SHOW that cocaine has approximately the same biochemical "signature" as happiness. It boosts the production of dopamine in your brain and gives you an intense feeling of euphoria. No wonder it is such an addictive drug. But it's not really because of the cocaine "rush" that it is so addictive—that wears off fairly quickly, once your brain gets used to the drug and stops getting fooled into producing dopamine. Instead, brain scans show that it is because the reward center in the brains of people who take cocaine is activated *before* they take the drug. Anticipation has a greater and longer-lasting effect than the drug itself.

There are two lessons to be learned from this. The first is: don't bother taking cocaine, because it's the pure anticipation that you're getting the rush from (you can, in other words, settle for the illusion). The second is that happiness actually works similarly: it gets going when you start to think about things you are looking forward to.

I have carried out studies of several thousand Swedes that show that we are a bit more likely to circle a higher number on the happiness scale on Fridays, because we are anticipating the weekend. Analyses of millions of posts on Twitter and the Chinese equivalent, Weibo, have revealed the same pattern. People say they are happiest on Fridays, as they look forward to the things they are going to do, but as soon as the weekend starts, the happiness curve turns downward again. So, we aren't happiest when it's the weekend and we are free to do the things we don't have time for during the week—but the day before, when we *think* most about those things.

In the same way, our vacations give us the most joy on the first day, when we relish all the things we are going to do (or not do). Then it quickly goes downhill, according to some investigations. For example, an American study found that 24% of couples who are flying away on vacation start arguing at the airport, while another study found that one in 10 relationships come to an end on vacation. In Sweden, filing for divorce peaks in August (I couldn't refrain from checking that).

If you ask German married couples, they'll tell you that they are a bit happier than average, but not as happy as couples who are engaged to be married. At least, that is what German researchers found when they measured the happiness of almost 100,000 people over several years.

So my advice is to forget all the pronouncements and words of wisdom you've ever heard about not claiming a premature victory, and instead do the opposite. Claim the victory before it's a fact and get the most of whatever you're looking forward to. Enjoy it while you have the chance—it will never turn out the way you expected anyway.

I've done a lot of research on people in all sorts of situations, and asked them make predictions about their next break, their next date, how well it'll go for their favorite team in the next game, how big a raise they're going to get, or what kind of physical condition they're going be in next year. Almost everybody thinks that more or less everything is going to be just great. I wrote a whole book about it: *Nextopia*.

It's the same reason that people who think the end of the world is close are happier—because they believe that something even better is coming. (Yes, researchers actually asked about it in that study. But they didn't think of asking *what* they actually expected would come.)

The future is a bit like sex: when it happens it's quicker than we would like and isn't really as good as we had fantasized. But we can't stop thinking about it; we do so several times a day.

You don't have to be a professor of economics to realize that it is a huge waste not to allow yourself to feel happiness when you think about an ideal future, while you wait around for a brief and worse version of future events to occur. If you declare victory in advance, then it won't matter if your team actually wins. And what's the worst that can happen? That you might be obliged to celebrate again if they do win? Because you can't really celebrate for no reason...

"Oh no! They didn't win! I've been happy all this time for no reason. It would have been so much better if I'd been unhappy *both now and all the time leading up to now.*"

That kind of thinking puts you at risk for depression. Clinical studies actually show that one of the most distinctive characteristics of people who suffer from depression is that they think less positively about the future. Not that they think less about the future—because like I've said, we can't refrain from thinking about the future—but less positively about it.

On the other hand, research shows that the people who think more positively about the future are a bit happier than average. What is distinct about those people is really not that they are more positive when they think about the future, because most of us do that completely automatically (with the exception of the unfortunate people who are depressed), but that they think *more* about the future.

Researchers call this "mental time travel," travelling in your thoughts to the events in the future you look forward to, and being really present there. See what it feels like: think about an event in the future; make it real inside your head as if it was truly happening. Does that sound silly?

Well, it isn't; it's all about synapses and neurons: the same neurons that store your experiences also store your fantasies. So, you can physically have memories both of things that have happened and things that haven't happened yet, as long as you experience it just as strongly in your mind. The same mechanism explains why witnesses sometimes testify in court that they saw something, when in fact they just happened to hear or read about it after the fact; for them, the memories feel just as true.

Researchers have carried out experiments where people have made mental time journeys to events they are looking forward to and found that they get a little happier right away. But what's interesting is that they were still a little happier *after* the actual events took place, even if they hadn't been as great as people had imagined (because, of course, they hardly ever are). The reason being that the early victory they'd declared was still present as a parallel memory.

But isn't there then a risk that I'll be disappointed? you might be thinking. That's the reason we've learned not to claim victory prematurely—so as not set our expectations too high. I have two answers to that. Firstly, you are going to be disappointed regardless (because if you aren't depressed, you simply can't prevent yourself from thinking positively). There will be "diminishing marginal returns," as the economists say, i.e., the disappointment doesn't increase at the same rate as the expectations. You won't, for example, be twice as disappointed about not getting a raise if you expected 1,000 crowns more than if you expected 500. Secondly, you only feel disappointment when the event actually takes place and that will be a shorter period than the time you've already spent celebrating your win.

I find that every time I leave the gym I'm thinking that the next time I'll set a personal weightlifting record. And I actually do it now and then, and then I really do celebrate (more about that later). But usually I don't (because if I did, I would spend my time travelling around the world being in different competitions, like the one where you have to fold books with your bare hands five times until they are the size of a postage stamp, instead of sitting at home and writing them). But I've barely left the gym before I've forgotten about my failed record attempt. Then I'm back to reveling in my expectations again, right up until the next gym session, and that's why I love working out (so much so that I stayed at home and wrote my previous book about it, *Starkt kul*).

Think about it the next time you are on your way to work or school: relish the great deeds you are going to accomplish. And when you go home, revel in the thought that it is going to be the best evening ever.

Then it doesn't matter if your boss is grumpy or the teacher is boring, or your family doesn't share your enthusiasm. You have had at least 15 minutes or half an hour of happiness that day, regardless of how it goes.

»THE FUTURE IS A BIT LIKE SEX:
WHEN IT HAPPENS IT'S QUICKER
THAN WE'D LIKE, AND ISN'T REALLY
AS GOOD AS WE'D FANTASIZED.«*

4

CELEBRATE

HAVE YOU ever woken up early in the morning, looked in the mirror, and been frightened to see your old mom or dad staring back at you? That's a reminder that, in the morning, you actually *are* a copy of your parents, at least as far as happiness is concerned. How happy you are when you wake up is determined by as much as 80% by your genes. But let me reassure you, at the end of the day your genes determine your happiness level by less than 40%.

Your happiness is hugely influenced by what you do during your day.

I measured the happiness of more than 1,000 Swedes one random morning and evening, and almost all of them showed changes in happiness level, up or down. The simplest way to explain these fluctuations was to count how many positive things (i.e., things that made them glad) and negative things (things that didn't make them glad) they had done during the day.

If you want to see your own smile in the mirror in the evening—instead of one of your parents—then my best tip is to celebrate things that make you happy.

That doesn't mean doing more of what makes you happy, but rather allowing yourself to enjoy more of what you already do. Take sex, for example. That's one of the daily (or nightly) things that people do that makes them happiest.

In an experiment, American researchers asked 100 or so married couples to double the number of times they had sex and measured their happiness over 3 months. It diminished.

It turned out that having more of it made these unfortunate couples enjoy sex less. (What's the optimal number of times to have sex a week, you might well be wondering. Well, there's research on that, too. A study of more than 30,000 people showed that sex was most enjoyable and had the most positive affect on people's happiness when it was engaged in once a week.)

So, what are you going to do the other days of the week? Perhaps celebrate that you have been together with your partner for 2 years, 3 months and 4 days? That only happens once in a relationship, and it's worth celebrating. Celebrate that you did well on a test or that it was a little easier when you went running this morning. Celebrate that you got your proposal approved at that meeting (or that the meeting was cancelled and you didn't have to go).

Every day there are things that bring you a little joy and when you celebrate them, can affect your happiness more than you'd think. There's a whole bunch of studies about this.

The first trick is to see them. It's a little like mindfulness: allow yourself to come to a stop for a moment when something happens, like when the teacher ends class 10 minutes *early* for once. That good fortune won't last long—next time they'll probably go 15 minutes over (we lecturers tend to do that, sorry...). But for that very reason, you ought to celebrate.

The whole point about celebrating, you see, is that it turns a negative (good fortune is fleeting) into something positive, by emphasizing how delightful it is when it actually happens—relishing the occurrence.

The other trick that happiness researchers recommend is to pay attention to what something feels like. To really savor the feeling. You might not be used to feeling delight in trivialities; it might even feel wrong. "This small thing isn't something to celebrate. It's not that amazing that I managed to do one push-up without my knees touching the ground." But when researchers asked people to celebrate their everyday life and record it in a diary, the diarists soon got in the habit of appreciating these little strokes of luck and tiny triumphs and their average happiness got a small bump throughout the period.

The third trick in using celebration to make yourself a little bit happier is to make a real show of it. *What will people think?* you might ask. They're going to think that it's fun for you, and your happiness is going to be contagious. High-five the people around you when you do that push-up and you'll see how the smiles spread across their faces, too. Text a friend and tell them, and I promise you that they will write something nice back, and maybe even suggest that you do something together to celebrate. If not, then I promise to do 100 push-ups myself (if you text me instead of that friend next time).

As several studies indicate, celebrating so that everyone can see makes both you and other people happier.

One final trick is to mark the thing that you're celebrating in some way. Have an ice cream in the middle of the day. Name a star; it isn't actually that expensive (there are lots of stars to choose from in the International Star Registry; if you can see the star from here, it will cost a few hundred bucks; stars further away are half the price). Carve something on a wooden bench in a nearby park (but don't say it was my idea if the authorities come knocking) or post something nice on Instagram. I haven't found a study that has tested any of these tricks, but researchers have, on the whole, given us carte blanche (it felt posh to employ a French phrase, rather than "free rein," to celebrate that I have almost finished writing this tip) to do just about anything at all to make the celebration a little bigger and a little longer-lasting.

Which leads me to the next tip:

Relive it!

This might seem a little unnecessary because it'll all be spelled out for you when you turn the next page, but now you have a few seconds to look forward to what you are going to learn about the experience of reliving something.

Enjoy!

»EVERY DAY THERE ARE
THINGS THAT BRING YOU A LITTLE JOY
AND WHEN YOU CELEBRATE THEM,
CAN AFFECT YOUR HAPPINESS
MORE THAN YOU'D THINK.«

5
RELIVE

IN THE early 20th century, nostalgia was seen as an illness. It was often called the "Swiss Illness," after the stories of Swiss mercenaries during the Crusades who became stricken with severe homesickness. The assumption was that people who suffer from nostalgia must have something wrong with their brains, because wanting to reexperience the past didn't seem to offer any logical benefits, other than making you a bit happier—and in the early 20th century, you'll recall, the benefits of happiness were regarded skeptically. Happiness itself was even considered to be abnormal.

It may not be that surprising that a person would be happier just by dreaming themselves back to a time before they headed off to war. But you can also raise your happiness levels by dreaming back, regardless of when you do it: just as most events are a bit better when you look forward to them than when they actually happen, events in the past are almost always a bit better when you reexperience and relive them in retrospect.

I have asked people to rate their happiness right after they've been envisioning a time 3 months or a year ahead, and after they've been thinking about a time just in the past. Most people's ratings assume a slightly uneven V-shape, with the future a bit higher than the past, and the present the low point. Not that the present moment is bad, but what we are look forward to and what we relive are even better. There is a similar pattern when people think about specific events. A trip we'll take, or one already taken, a past or future date: they all appear better than the present.

So my tip is not only to declare an early victory—declare a postdated one, too.

One reason why we aren't happier when events are actually happening is that we don't have the time to. The present—*the now*—is so short. It's not just that dinner or a date might be short in itself—research on the way people experience time shows that we find it difficult to think about *the now* for very long—our thoughts just keep moving. We experience the present time, what is going on *right here and right now* only a few seconds at a time (approximately four) while our thoughts dart back and forth.

That doesn't allow much time for celebrating, does it?

Happiness researchers talk about reliving experiences as a form of time travel, which enables you to go back in time and see and enjoy events you didn't really have time to appreciate when they were going on. The human brain is fantastic that way; it can store information and memories that you weren't ever really aware of. Not only can you celebrate victory in retrospect, again and again, each time getting a little happiness bump to reexperience some wonderful event, but you can actually experience *more* of the event and see new things afterwards. You might not even have perceived it as a victory when it happened, but afterwards you see things that make the event worth celebrating.

It's never too late to have a happy childhood.

This particular concept has worked for me, actually. There were lots of things I wished were different when I was growing up, and at the time all I wanted was to escape. But since I started going back and reexperiencing certain parts of it, I've discovered and noticed things that I couldn't see the value in at the time, things that now make me happy.

Our memory is so ingenious that it likes to make a sort of "greatest hits compilation" of events as it's storing them. You select those bits which have the best potential to make you happy when you think about them, and you place them right at the front of your mental photo album.

No wonder after people in experiments are asked to reexperience events earlier in their lives, they proceed to circle a somewhat higher figure on the happiness scale. Or that people who in general are a bit more nostalgic and liable to make mental time journeys are a bit happier than average.

That is one of the explanations why, as research shows, our happiness increases slightly when we get older: we have more events and victories to celebrate, over and over again.

It can also explain why the feeling of happiness changes over the years, from something linked to excitement and elation to something experienced more as warmth, calm, and security, based on the rich store of events you can choose from to re-experience.

As a bonus, you will also grow more optimistic about the future by celebrating your victories in retrospect: *Things went so well for me before, why shouldn't they again?* Research shows that when making predictions about the outcome of an upcoming event—whether in sports, in school, or on a date—people who think back to similar, earlier experiences tend to anticipate greater success.

It's as good as a Kinder Surprise egg, that Swiss illness.

»NOSTALGIC PEOPLE ARE A BIT HAPPIER THAN THE AVERAGE.«

6

INDULGE YOURSELF

MY GREAT-GRANDFATHER was awakened every night by his poodle, Billy. The poodle knew that he had kept chocolate in the drawer of his bedside table, and at the first sign of light (which is sometime before 3:00 a.m. on Swedish summer nights), Billy would poke him until he finally opened the drawer and pulled out two pieces of chocolate, one for Billy and one for himself (against recommendations of both his doctor and the vet).

This went on as long as I can remember. Great-grandpa's health was already a little dicey at 70 years old, when I was born, but he lived to the age of 93. And Billy, for his part, lived to 98 in dog years.

I think about them sometimes. Great-Grandpa, Billy, and the chocolate pieces.

I thought about them while comparing the happiness and the dietary habits of a few thousand Swedes and discovered that flexitarians, people who primarily have a plant-based diet but sometimes eat animal products, turned out to be a bit happier than all the others (without having to remind themselves, like the vegans). The explanation is presumably that they indulge themselves: sometimes they're vegetarian, sometimes they eat meat, but above all, they eat candy and chips. The study revealed that flexitarians were twice as likely to visit the aisles with the chips and candy bins in the supermarket (I guess to balance out being responsible and having such a balanced diet).

Being responsible all the time isn't much fun. Just ask any kid. Researchers have done just that, asked everyone from American preschool children to college students in the Philippines. They found that children sometimes did the opposite of what the teacher said, just because it was fun, and that students who, for example, took an extra-long break or simply skipped some schoolwork, felt a bit happier (and with that, I suppose I've reduced the likelihood of this book being used in schools to zero).

It works the same with adult children. In an Australian study, when just over 1,000 people were asked the question whether they sometimes did "naughty" things, more than 80% answered yes. The majority did them to feel happier and because it made them feel young. This applied to all age groups but was most common among people in their 30s.

The most common "naughty" behavior was to buy something they didn't really need, to call in "sick" from work (and with that, there's now no risk that employers will be buying this book for their employees), or skip some household chore.

I saw a similar effect when I asked a few hundred former students to skip something every day that they didn't want to do and write diaries about how it went. Not only did they all survive (some were slightly worried at first), but as they gradually got used to occasionally skipping a meeting or not showing up for their time slot at the laundromat (a cardinal sin here in Sweden), their daily happiness increased a little. Most of them kept their job and family, too (yeah, I'm joking, they all did).

Personally, I'm extremely fond of a popular Swedish Christmas candy called Juleskum, a fluffy two-colored strawberry-flavored marshmallow Santa made by Cloetta. In my home country, I'm kind of notorious for munching on these marshmallow Santas all year round (I have my own Santa stash in the basement).

"But that's no fun!" some people object. "If you eat them all year, then they're not special. The whole point is wait until Christmas!" But for me that is the whole point; I enjoy eating them when it *isn't* Christmas. They rarely taste better than in the summer. And they really never taste as good as when somebody tells me again that it's wrong, that I'm missing the point and the pleasure of these Christmas goodies. But I don't let myself get distracted by these criticisms; I eat three marshmallow Santas a day and enjoy them every time.

Now, I am not implying that everybody would be happier by eating marshmallow Santas in the summer. For some people it really might take the pleasure out of these Christmas candies and even out of Christmas itself (but in that case, they might want to rethink how they do Christmas), and I have heard that there are even people who don't like marshmallows at all.

My point is quite simply:

Find your own marshmallow Santa.

By which I mean something that you give yourself for no reason. Not for Christmas, or workouts or a school test, or a birthday. Not in celebration of anything (we've already covered how to do that in an earlier chapter).

It can be pretty much anything. An ice cream, a leisurely walk with your favorite music playing in your headphones, an extended break—it can vary from day to day. Maybe a little a fling outside of your relationship? (Well, that last one might not be a good idea. Researchers have actually found that the optimal number of sexual partners is one, after that the "marginal utility" is negative, to speak like an economist. Besides, most people who are unfaithful suffer from guilt or stress about being found out, which has a negative effect on their happiness. But I allowed myself to write that tip simply to enjoy the image of you spitting out your coffee when you read it!)

Studies show that people who have a greater tendency to indulge themselves, to allow themselves things in everyday life, are a bit happier on average. Researchers found that when they encouraged people to allow themselves various little treats (for example, an outing or something tasty to eat) for a few days, those people were slightly more satisfied with life after that period than they were beforehand.

In a fun experiment—fun at least for us who didn't have to participate—some students were given a math test, others weren't, and all were told they could take as many chocolate truffles as they wanted, regardless of whether they had taken the test or not. It turned out that those students who took the test and took a few more chocolate truffles felt happier about passing the test than those who took fewer (because they had celebrated). Those who took more truffles but did not take the test also felt a bit happier (because they had indulged themselves).

The researchers saw the same pattern when they told students at random that they had done better or worse on the test: those who believed they did well felt they'd celebrated their success by taking more truffles, while those who believed that they hadn't done well felt a bit happier when they indulged in some extra chocolates.

It works out whether you're good at math or not.
Or in more general terms: celebrate when you have a reason to, and indulge yourself for no reason at all.

It doesn't even have to be with something you like. Try ice cream with béarnaise sauce and you'll see. It's disgusting. That was why I started eating it, as a test to see if I could get used to the taste within a week.

And during that week, I ate ice cream with béarnaise sauce several times a day in all sorts of situations and noticed pretty quickly that I did actually become a bit happier each time, not because I got used to the taste (which I admittedly did in the end), but because I enjoyed indulging myself in such a disgusting, unnecessary activity. After I reported the results on television, I heard several times from people who had ordered béarnaise sauce to go with their ice cream at restaurants, ice cream parlors, and even dinner parties—not because it is tasty (it truly is disgusting, unless you eat it several times a day for a week to get used to it) but to indulge themselves in a weird pleasure.

»CELEBRATE WHEN YOU HAVE A REASON TO, AND INDULGE WHEN YOU HAVE NO REASON AT ALL.«

7

GET SOME EXERCISE

IN GERMANY they have *Tanzverbot*, a ban on dancing, on Good Friday and All Saints' Day. The fear is that dancing will put people in a particularly good mood, which would be inappropriate on these serious holidays. It might sound weird, but the same ban exists in Switzerland, and has been in place in a bunch of other countries on different holidays over the years. Up until 2016, special permission was necessary in Sweden to dance in places that served alcohol. The ban on dancing goes back to the 17th century, when they already had an inkling as to what happiness research would ascertain several hundred years later: you do indeed become a bit happier just from moving your body. In Sweden we even have a special word for this: *rörelseglädje*, literally "the joy of moving."

It doesn't have to be dancing or any other uninhibited activity that many associate with the word. Just taking the stairs instead of taking the escalator up from the subway will suffice. When we talked to a few hundred people who had come up out of a subway station, those who had taken the stairs were on average a bit happier.

It could, of course, have been that the people who were already happier also had more energy and therefore took the stairs, while those who were less happy chose to mope along on the escalator. This would certainly fit with the research showing that people who are more optimistic are also more likely to engage in physical exercise and sports.

So, we tested this by randomly approaching people at the Central Railway Station in Stockholm and asking them to circle a number on the happiness scale, either on the spot or while we walked with them for a bit. And we got the same results: those who assessed their happiness while walking felt a little happier on average.

An explanation for why something as simple as taking the stairs or walking along for a short distance makes you happier is that it makes your heart beat faster, and happiness and heart rate work together. Researchers have asked people to relive happy memories or to watch a film that makes them happy and observed that their pulse increases in conjunction with their score on the happiness scale. Perhaps we unconsciously associate a faster pulse with feeling happy, so that it works in the opposite direction too: is an increased pulse in itself enough to raise someone's happiness level?

We tested this by asking almost 100 people to ride exercise bikes at various degrees of resistance, got their heart rates up quickly, and then asked them to circle how happy they felt. On average they rated themselves higher on the scale when they had a faster pulse.

Another explanation for why you feel a bit happier from getting some exercise is that it literally gives you a warmer feeling in your body. Researchers have measured the temperature of people's faces and fingers and found that they become a bit warmer when they are happy. Just like with your heart rate, it seems to work in the opposite direction too: when a group of retirees engaged in physical exercise, their experienced happiness increased regardless of what they did, but it increased least when they went swimming (lowest body temperature), most when they did weight training (highest body temperature), and somewhere in the middle when they went for a walk.

When you get some exercise, you also enjoy a cocktail of released hormones, such as endorphins and dopamine which are usually called "happiness hormones." You've heard of "runner's high," the feeling of euphoria you get from strenuous effort? It's real: there is research which shows that you can become addicted to that rush, just like you would any other drug (but don't worry—as long as you don't go tractor-pulling a truck or running a marathon every day, you won't be at risk).

Moreover, when you exercise, you often get a little boost of sex hormones, which have a positive effect on your sense of well-being (and which also explains why so many people get flirty whey they go to a gym). You also get growth hormones, which build and repair your body, and serotonin, which makes you sleep better (and the quality of your sleep has a great influence on your mood).

This can help explain why exercise is found to have positive effects on happiness in studies ranging from Danish children to middle-aged Koreans and Iranian retirees, on high school athletes, as well as disabled people, and cancer patients. By getting your body to feel a little better, you'll make your head feel a little better.

A Norwegian study even found that exercise during your youth isn't just an investment in a healthy body, with effects that can carry through the rest of your life, but it's also an investment in happiness for the rest of your life. The researchers found that young people who exercised more eventually became slightly happier adults, regardless of whether they continued exercising more than others (which most of them did) or not (when researchers adjusted mathematically for that absence in their analysis).

But physical activity is above all a renewable resource. An epidemiological study which measured the exercise habits of more than 17,000 Canadians over 15 years found that when they increased their average daily exercise (measured as the number of calories burnt per kilo of body weight), their happiness increased, too, and when their exercise decreased, their happiness level also went down.

The same phenomenon could be seen in a study of 10,000 Swedes who had activity trackers installed on their phones. The trackers measured how much the phones (and therefore the person who had the phone on them) moved. They were asked at random times of the day to circle a figure on the happiness scale, which was then cross-checked with the reported movement in the phone during the previous quarter of an hour. The numbers were, on average, a bit higher when the person had just been physically active.

Accordingly, my advice is this: get some exercise. Anything at all, any time at all; it doesn't make much difference. Whatever exercise you do, you will become a bit happier. Every day.

If you commute to work, maybe you can bike or walk. There is a Swedish study which shows that people are actually happier when they have further to commute to their job, if that means they do more physical activity to get there.

Do a few dance moves when nobody's watching (or better yet, when somebody *is* watching, as that will make them happier, too). Kill two birds with one stone and do it on Good Friday or another holiday. Take the stairs instead of the escalator or the elevator at some point during the day. Get a workout in during your lunch break and feel how your endorphins and happiness hormones go through the roof. Or simply walk a few steps around your office and feel a tiny bit happier.

The joy of physical activity comes in many forms and can be tapped into every day.

»THE RESEARCHERS FOUND THAT YOUNG PEOPLE WHO GOT A LITTLE MORE EXERCISE WERE ALSO SLIGHTLY HAPPIER IN ADULTHOOD.«

8
GET IN THE FLOW

IN 1992, Ozzy Osbourne travelled around the world on his retirement tour, *No More Tears, No More Tours*, saying that, at 44 years old, he didn't want to turn into some pathetic old man onstage. Three years later, he was back onstage again, stating, "Retirement sucks."

Fast-forward 25 years and he'd done two more farewell tours and declared onstage again as a 70-year-old that he would probably never stop, since it was the only thing he was good at.

No amount of money or drugs (Ozzy has obviously had plenty of both) seems to be able to beat the feeling of doing something you're good at. Ask Tina Turner or Cher, who've also done their fair share of farewell tours. Or Keith Richards, who, in an almost mummified state, time after time goes out on the road with the Rolling Stones—and between tours plays in obscure jazz and blues bands, just because he loves playing the guitar.

It just feels good to be good.

Happiness researchers call it being in a flow state. People in a flow state are a little happier than other people.

That might not come as a shock: you've probably had that great feeling yourself at one time or another, when everything is going your way and it seems as if you can't do anything wrong. But you probably associate the feeling with luck. Curiously, the Swedish word for flow, *flyt*—just like the word "happiness" originally—is synonymous with "luck."

But as Swedish skier Ingemar Stenmark, who won multiple Olympic and World Cup medals, famously said: "I don't know anything about luck. I just know that the more I train, the more luck I have." It's the same with flow. The better you are at doing something, the greater the flow you'll have when you do it.

That applies just as much to skiing as to playing the guitar. Or cooking, solving math problems, playing computer games, climbing mountains, or managing projects. For all those activities, there is research which shows that you can experience flow state if you are good at doing them.

Researchers have asked people to circle a figure on the happiness scale at random times of the day and write down what they are doing at the time and found that higher ratings coincide with being in flow state, regardless of what the subjects were doing.

What all these events have in common is that they have a perfect balance between being challenging and being manageable. It's like skiing down a steep slope which you can just about handle, or experimenting with a new dish which demands all your skills in the kitchen. Going down the bunny slope (unless you are a child—but then, presumably, you wouldn't be reading this book—or unless you're skiing for the very first time) or warming up a can of ravioli (with the same caveats about being a child or cooking for the first time) is just boring. And mogul skiing can feel more like a death wish if you don't have proper control (while trying out a new dish without the requisite skills doesn't have quite the same stakes, it can still be pretty stressful).

The better you become, the greater the challenges you dare to take on and the more control you feel you have—and that's how flow increases.

There are several reasons why the flow state feels so good and makes you happier. It is not entirely surprising that it's rewarding to be good at something, and it increases your self-confidence to know that you can deal with challenges. It increases your creativity, too. As we saw at the beginning of the book, happy people are a bit more creative, and people who are creative are a bit happier. These are basic evolutionary-reward systems, which make us feel better when we are good at something and when we are creative, so that we will keep on developing and increasing our chances of survival.

Being in a flow state also means that we're absorbed in what we're doing. You've heard a sportscaster say that someone in a flow state is "in the zone," which is quite a good description:

flow takes you into your own time zone and geography, where you are no longer aware of time passing and what is happening around you. All the things that might otherwise bother you fall away, out of sight—no worrying about something you did or what somebody else might be doing or thinking. You get a little break from everything that can submerge your happiness, and it pops up to the surface like a cork.

The flow state is, in a way, an efficient variety of mindfulness that makes you more present in what you're doing and lets you enjoy it. Personally, I have always been terrible at mindfulness and fretted that I should be doing it (that is, nothing, and just focusing on the here and now). And I would worry about how bad I was at just concentrating on breathing or whatever it might be. But when I started looking into the mechanisms of the flow state, I realized that it is precisely because *I'm not good at those things* that I can't do mindfulness. When, however, I do things that I *am* good at—for example when I do chin-ups or differential equations—it's different.

Those examples might not be perfect; there probably aren't that many people who share my propensity to get into the flow by hanging from a bar or juggling numbers. But that's exactly the point about the flow state—it can come in any form whatsoever. It's entirely up to you and what you're good at.

Getting into the flow state is the answer to the question *What's the point of doing that?* Which someone may have asked, or you may have asked yourself, when you sit inside and play computer games, hike deep into the forest to hang off a mountain wall, or sit and draw giraffe after giraffe after giraffe. It's because you are good at it and it feels good.

Flow can of course be extremely useful in and of itself. Studies show that flow at your work means you perform better and are more satisfied with your job, and that flow in school makes students learn more and like learning better. That's why it is an excellent idea to try to create flow in these contexts that you devote a lot of time to and which are important parts of your life. Give yourself challenges, train yourself to master them, and know that you are good at what you do.

But my most important tip is to do what you are good at. Regardless of what it is. There are no pathetic old rock stars onstage, just happy artistes. And there is no bad flow state; there's just flow. Take a little time for yourself now and then to feel good by being good at something. On your guitar, on the ski slope, or in front of your computer screen. A computer game isn't a waste of time if it lets you experience flow and feel a little happier. And if you're a bit happier, we know that it will affect the other things you do. Perhaps ward off a cold and reduce the number of days you miss work or school, or make you a bit more creative in that project you're working on. And just maybe it will give you more luck in court (but, like I said, I hope you will never need that kind of luck).

»THERE ARE NO PATHETIC
OLD ROCK STARS ONSTAGE,
JUST HAPPY ARTISTES.«

9

BE NiCE

BEING CALLED nice might not seem like something to write home about. "Nice boys don't get to kiss beautiful girls," a Swedish saying goes (but nobody says whether they get to kiss beautiful boys). "Good girls go to heaven; bad girls go everywhere else," iconic film star Mae West used to say. I haven't found any research pertaining to what the real deal is with kisses, but an American study which was recently carried out on more than 2,000 speed-dating singles showed that men who were seen as nice got more yeses. The same held true for women. Both, however, earn less money (according to another American study which cross-checked the appraised niceness and income of more than 4,000 men and women). So being nice doesn't make you richer—but it does make you and others happier.

The fact is that treating others like you want to be treated works. Literally. At least when it comes to being nice.

In a Canadian study, researchers gave 2-year-olds a bowl of cookies and measured their facial expressions when they would eat one (because it was kind of hard to ask them to circle a number on the happiness scale). Not surprisingly, they were beaming. Then the researchers tried holding a bowl of cookies and letting a new gang of 2-year-olds take one out of the bowl and feed it to a cookie-eating doll (yes, that's right, they had programmed the doll with cookie-munching sounds). The children's faces lit up in the same way. When they did the experiment a third time, they gave the 2-year-olds the bowl and explained that the cookies were theirs and that they could choose to give their own cookies to the doll; all the children gave away a cookie. The warm glow on their faces was even a little brighter when they gave away their own cookies, rather than when they picked cookies out of the researchers' bowls.

A "warm glow" is actually what happiness researchers call their explanation for why people choose to be kind without expecting anything in return.

When we give something to another person (or a cookie-munching doll), it feels as if we are getting the same thing ourselves; you can see a warm glow on children's faces as well as adults' (if you measure really carefully, which is something happiness researchers like doing). Neurological studies have found that the warm glow also occurs in the part of the brain which reacts to getting rewards. You don't even need to see the person you are giving something to, or know who they are, for that matter; researchers have seen exactly the same neurological effects when people donate money to charity. When you are kind to others, you're just as happy as when other people are kind to you. That's pretty cool, right?

A plus here is that it increases the likelihood that others will treat you kindly in return. When children in 19 Canadian middle school classes were given an assignment three times a week to either go on fun little outings or do acts of kindness, they circled slightly higher numbers on the happiness scale on average when queried 4 weeks later, regardless of which they had done. But those who had been kind also reported that their friends had been kinder to them and that they felt more liked.

In other words, being kind makes you a little happier in the short term, as well as the long term. First you get to enjoy the experience of being kind to others (which feels like it's happening to you), and then you get to experience others actually becoming friendlier to you.

That might explain why kind people live longer. When researchers collated studies which had been carried out in the US, Europe, and Asia on people of every possible age, they found that those who regularly helped others (for example as volunteers, or helping older neighbors mow the lawn) were twice as likely to live 5 years longer. They also need half as much medical care, on average.

Australian researchers ascertained this when they were asked to find solutions to the long waits for treatment at psychiatric clinics in England. As people waited to start therapy for various mental problems, they were given prescriptions to do good deeds. After 2 weeks, many of the patients on the waiting list reported that they felt better from having been kind while they waited. Some felt so good that they didn't even need therapy any longer.

This all sounds fantastic, of course, but perhaps you shouldn't count on everything in life sorting itself out just because you're kind now and then—that you'll be happy and liked by all, have eternal life, and not need therapy.

But it isn't a bad idea at all to count on kindness. People who count the number of times they have been kind in the past week do tend to feel happier. This is a typical intervention method, which is a fancy term for a way for get people to behave or think differently.

Counting is a simple way of reminding yourself and making yourself aware of something, and people who remind themselves of when they have been kind become a bit happier, which makes them a little more likely to do kind things again. Happiness researchers call this a "positive feedback loop."

So the only question is, in what way you should be kind? Hand out cookies, donate money to charity, take the money you got from an unexpected bonus to buy something for somebody else (yes, there's research on that, too)? Any of these will do, though kindness doesn't have to involve money of course (there just happen to be a lot of studies about money). You can hold the door for somebody, give them a compliment, run after somebody with a glove they dropped on the street, or leave a book you finished reading on the train with a little message to the person who finds it. It can be completely random things.

As long as you do it to make somebody else happy, it works.

But how do I know if it's going to make somebody else happy? you might be wondering. Well, to use a cliché, you know it when you see it (the same way as with other things, like if you're in love, or if you've soiled yourself—you just know). The Swedish word for "nice," *snäll*, originally meant "fast" (as in the German *schnell*, which explains why express trains in Sweden are called *snälltåg*) and were used when you needed help fast: "*Snäll*, help me!"). So being *snäll* means knowing how you can be of help and make somebody happy.

So how can you be so sure? Because you feel that whatever it is would make you happy if you were in the other person's shoes. That also helps explain the meaning of "kind" in English, which also signifies "the same type" or "similar." It is so simple that 2-year-olds get it. Even chimpanzees seem to know how they can make people happy. That, at least, is how researchers explain why the chimpanzees they study try to console them when they are feeling down, although they won't go as far as to give away their bananas to make someone happy (of course that has been tested too, in a variety of ways, but that seems to be where chimps draw the line).

The researchers conclude that we humans seem to have a stronger link than the chimps between the warm glow of happiness and being kind. I personally think that the chimps simply have a stronger link between the warm glow of happiness and eating bananas themselves.

»PEOPLE WHO COUNT THE NUMBER OF TIMES THEY HAVE BEEN KIND IN THE PAST WEEK DO TEND TO FEEL HAPPIER. THE EFFECTS ARE EXACTLY THE SAME WHEN PEOPLE DONATE MONEY TO CHARITY.«

10
BE GRATEFUL

THE SUN nearly always shines in California. The Pacific Ocean sparkles along the coast and maintains roughly the same temperature year-round in the sunshine. The palms sway in the sea breeze along the boulevards. The sun loves California, as Beth Hart sings in the soundtrack to the series *Californication.*

But Californians aren't any happier for it.

You'd think they would be, walking around and looking cool in their sunglasses. But studies show that the sun and good weather, on the whole, don't have any effect on their happiness. They take their delightful weather for granted. As opposed to us Swedes, who really do know how to appreciate the sun, when it finally shows itself. When I measured 1,000 randomly chosen people's happiness across the country and cross-checked the results with the weather where they were, it turned out that those who found themselves in places where the sun was shining circled a slightly higher number on the scale.

We are far too quick to take things for granted. Health, for example. How often are you happy about not being ill? Probably almost never, even though it is the most basic condition for you to be able to feel good and do what makes you happy. The only times we seem to realize that are when we are sick or injured and wish more than anything that we could be healthy again. That's why colds are just great—they remind us not to take health for granted. When I measured happiness in people who had recently had a cold, they were a bit happier than average. Unfortunately, the lovely feeling of not having a cold goes away within a few days or, at most, a week.

So, my advice is: **Be more appreciative!**

The main reason why most of us aren't happier is not that we're lacking anything, but that we don't *think* about how good we have it.

That is the reason why, as I mentioned in the introductory chapter, we can't experience happiness peaks for longer than 3 months. It seems that is the limit to how long it takes to become accustomed to things and start to take them for granted, however fantastic they may be. Raises, promotions, winning the lottery, love, family—however great the joy when they happen, in 3 months, we have grown accustomed to them.

So the first thing we need to do to appreciate the fantastic things in our lives is to remind ourselves of them.

I think of this as giving ourselves a kind of mental cold now and then, as a way of reminding ourselves of how lovely it is to be healthy (and what's so great about this is that people who are a bit happier are also less likely to get a cold, so if you remind yourself what it feels like to have a cold, and how delightful it is that you actually don't have a cold, you're going to also reduce the risk of getting a cold for real, which is pretty nice!).

This even works for Californians, who aren't happier than us Swedes, despite the fact that they live in the climate of our dreams. If you remind Californians that they actually live in California, as some of my colleagues did, they end up higher on the scale of happiness.

I got a tattoo of a tractor on my foot that was run over a few years ago, and every time I see the tractor I do actually feel a bit happier that my foot is no longer as flat as a pancake and that I no longer have to hobble around with a huge boot.

The other suggestion that happiness researchers have for making us a bit happier based on the great things we have in life is literally to express that we are grateful.

You can go as far as keeping a gratitude diary where, at the end of every day, you write down the things you are grateful for. Several studies have shown that within a week or so of starting this practice, people begin to circle slightly higher figures on the happiness scale and even report that they are less stressed—and sleep and feel better. That's a smart way of reminding yourself to be attentive and grateful. But as long as you can remember to think about it, it's enough just to think the thought. In experiments where people were asked to think about something for which they are grateful, researchers observed that people's heart rate went up slightly and that they showed the same physical symptoms as people experiencing little happiness peaks.

Another strategy is simply to say "thank you" when somebody does something kind. It doesn't have to be anything big—it can be passing the salt or holding open the door—the point is to show that you don't take the deed for granted. Or you can thank someone just because that person is there in your life. It takes less than a second to say those two words—thank you—but it has been shown to make both the person who says it and the person who hears it feel a little better the rest of the day.

A third strategy for being grateful for what you have is to refrain from comparing yourself to others.

Because comparisons are one of the surest ways to stop appreciating what you have yourself. Take sex once a week as an example: as you might remember, that is the number of times per week that makes married couples happiest. When (sadistic?) researchers point out to couples who have sex once a week that there are others who have sex more often, they immediately become less happy with their (optimally happy!) conjugal life.

The same applies to the number of partners and children (oh yes, there is research on that, too). As soon as people hear about others who have more, then their happiness about the number they have themselves sinks (people's happiness is at its highest with one partner, peaks at one child, and then plateaus). And this, of course, also applies to money, things, and everything you can think of. Researchers even carried out a study of commuters who became less happy when they compared their own commute with others'.

And the icing on the cake: gratitude has been shown to make people less materialistic. Because there *is* so much more to be grateful for than mere things. (The professor in me immediately has a sudden urge to get people to write a gratitude list before Christmas and then see if their wish list gets shorter.)

If you feel like writing your own gratitude list but don't really know where and how to begin, here are a few tips from a study from the Netherlands which analyzed the content of the gratitude lists of just over 400 people.

The five most common themes turned out to be:

→ Other people. "My friend who I had a coffee with today," "My clumsy adult child who always makes me feel needed."

→ Health: "My bad back didn't hurt so much today," "I reached my goal when I went running," "My foot wasn't run over by a tractor today." (OK, that last one crept in from a Swedish professor of economics.)

- → Work: "I'm doing a really fun project," "They treated us to muffins today," "They loved my presentation."

- → Environment: "The sun was shining all day" (the weather in the Netherlands is roughly the same as in Sweden), "The smell of newly cut grass," "They finally put a roof on the bus shelter so that I didn't have to get rained on." (Did I mention that they have roughly the same weather as Sweden?)

- → Leisure activities: "Petting my cat," "The good book that I read," "I had time for a bike ride before it got dark."

As for me, at this second, I am grateful that you'll soon turn the page and read the next chapter, because that chapter is my personal favorite and it makes me happy to think about what you'll make of it.

Thanks in advance!

»THE MAIN REASON WHY MOST OF US AREN'T HAPPIER IS NOT THAT THINGS AREN'T GOING WELL ENOUGH FOR US, BUT THAT WE DON'T THINK ABOUT HOW GOOD WE HAVE IT.«

11

BE TOGETHER

WHEN JON Snow was betrayed and killed by his brothers in the Night's Watch in the fifth season of *Game of Thrones*, Twitter was flooded with almost 700,000 tweets from people all over the world who needed to work through the shock. Researchers who analyzed the tweets found that they showed the same phases of denial, anger, negotiation, depression, and finally acceptance that people go through when they mourn the death of a loved one.

Jon Snow might have been a made-up character, but people's sorrow over his fate and their need to share their feelings with others were completely genuine.

A feeling of community arose among these hundreds of thousands of mourners.

In South Korea, hundreds of thousands of viewers gather in front of screens at dinnertime every evening to watch *muk-bang*, the popular eating shows or "eatcasts" (a portmanteau of "eating" and "broadcast"): people film themselves eating and broadcast it live on YouTube and other channels. The phenomenon has grown in line with the number of one-person households in the country, which is people sitting alone at home in the evenings without anybody to share a meal with. They are not only hungry for food, but also for somebody to share it with, so they eat dinner in the company of the "eatcast" onscreen. Because food does of course taste better when you have someone to share it with.

Just like most things in life.

Shared sorrow, like that over the death of Jon Snow, is said to cut the sorrow in half, and shared joy is doubled joy. Unfortunately, the latter isn't exactly correct. But it isn't very far from the truth. Shared joy is more like one and two-thirds joy, at least if shared with a friend within a one-mile radius.

Let me explain.

In a study that followed almost 5,000 people in New England over a period of 20 years, the researchers observed that when a person became happier, the likelihood that their friends would also become happier increased by 63%. Which is delightful, isn't it? Happiness is infectious. And it doesn't stop there. Happiness continues to infect in another two steps: when a close friend becomes a bit happier, it increases the likelihood that you will become a bit happier, which in turn increases the likelihood that your other close friends will become a bit happier, which in turn increases the likelihood that their close friends will become a bit happier (by all of 8%, which isn't bad at all, considering that they don't even know you or the friend who first made you happier).

Sharing happiness is one of our most fundamental mental functions. Already at the age of 4 months, as soon as our eyesight develops and we start to see clearly, our gaze is automatically drawn to smiling faces. If you measure the brain activity of babies at that age (yes, researchers have even done that) you can see how the same reward areas are triggered as when we adults circle higher figures on the happiness scale.

The same applies to baristas. If you smile at a barista you get a little happier. Not because he or she is a barista, but because researchers have tested whether the effects of smiling (and thereby sharing a bit of happiness) works regardless of whether you know the person you are smiling at, and regardless of the situation—and they found that it does, even when you order a coffee from a stranger in a busy café.

Smiles create a sense of community, and the feeling of being together makes us happy. Researchers have measured people's automatic tendency to smile while they watch funny videos, and in a follow-up 6 months later, observed that those who were more inclined to smile also felt a greater sense of community with other people during the past months—and they were happier.

Give life a smile, and life will smile back at you.

And you don't actually need to smile. It suffices to look another person in the eye to feel a sense of community. Try it, and you'll see. A second or two is all it takes for another person to feel seen and for both of you to sense that you share the same context.

The difference between seeing and not seeing each other is greater than most of us are aware of. In an experiment, students got to circle a number on the scale of happiness after having walked through campus, unaware that all the students they passed had been asked to look them—or not look them—in the eye. Those who were seen rated their happiness a little higher on average than those who weren't seen, without even being aware of it when they were asked.

I really did feel what a big difference it makes when one day I dressed up as a homeless person and sat in a pedestrian area in the middle of the city. During the hours I sat there, thousands of people passed by and almost nobody looked at me; it was as if I wasn't there. Before that, I'd taken for granted the sense of community that gets strengthened for a second now and then when we meet one another's gaze. And now there I was, sitting on the same street that I had walked only the previous day, and felt as if I was somewhere completely different, completely alone. Since then, I remind myself every day about the experience and what it does to look other people in the eye and how little it takes:

Count to three and see other people become happier.

It doesn't take any longer than that. After 3 seconds your eyes have said all you need to say: we are here together (if you want to look longer, you can of course do so, but clinical studies show that the effect doesn't become stronger and that some people even think it begins to feel uncomfortable around the fourth second.)

Smiles and gazes presume that we can actually see each other, and that helps explain why shared joy increases by two-thirds when you share it somebody within a one-mile radius. Maybe you're wondering about the proximity? It comes from that study of almost 5,000 people in New England, carried out between 1983 and 2003. That means it was during a time before the Internet or cellphones, and so people needed to be together (and an English mile was a nice round figure to measure distance in; if they had measured in Swedish kilometers the conclusion would certainly have been quite different).

But now there's the Internet and we have cellphones. And being together there works, too. Researchers analyzed 60 million Twitter users' activity and found that a happy tweet was infectious to those who read it and increased the likelihood that they in turn tweeted something happy, which then spread yet another step. It didn't have the same impact as physical meetings, but the "happiness infection" was nevertheless evident. What's so great about the Internet is that it also means that you can become friends and get together with more people.

For someone like me, who is shy and didn't have many friends growing up, it is absolutely fantastic to get so many friends. It is something I had never even dreamed of. I become a bit happier every time I enter my social media and see the number of friends I have.

Studies of this effect have found that friends on Facebook make people happier. To a certain point, anyway. The link is U-shaped, so that happiness first increases and then, when you have too many friends, it goes down a bit. The reason for this is that the sense of connection to friends feels weaker and weaker after a certain point, so that they, in the worst case, start to feel like an anonymous public, which gives you performance anxiety, or like the strangers that we compare ourselves with and become jealous of (you remember the previous chapter, don't you?).

Personally it makes me happy to have so many friends and that every morning I have a whole bunch that I can send birthday greetings to. Every greeting makes me a bit happier, as I feel that I get to be a part of someone's life. It is a fantastic feeling to hear back and know that I've shared a little of their big day, even though we might never have met.

Try it yourself: send a message to somebody you think about and see what happens. I usually ask people to do that before I start my lectures. Almost everybody ends up getting happy answers back before the end of the lecture, and when I ask students to raise their hands if they feel happier, almost every hand goes up.

So, my tip is:

Be together with other people every day.

Socialize for a while with family and friends. Smile at a barista. Look somebody in the eye and stop being strangers to each other. Let somebody know that you're thinking about them. It makes a bigger difference than you think, for both of you.

Does it work with squirrels and trees, too? you might be wondering. It's a good question, and I'm happy to tell you that a study has been carried out which shows that people who feel a strong affinity with nature also feel a bit happier.

»JOY THAT IS SHARED
GROWS BY TWO-THIRDS WHEN YOU
SHARE IT WITH SOMEBODY WITHIN
A ONE-MILE RADIUS.«

12
BE YOURSELF

BE YOURSELF; everybody else is already taken.

It is very easy to say (and quite a few people have, since Oscar Wilde famously came up with the adage in the late 1800s), and it makes a nice meme on Instagram, but to actually *be* yourself is really damn difficult. Not even the richest people in the world—people who otherwise don't seem to see any obstacles or limitations whatsoever in their lives (which helps if you are going to be one of the world's richest people)—manage it particularly well. Some persistent happiness researchers managed to get 49 people from the *Forbes* list of the world's richest people to circle numbers on the happiness scale and found that they did indeed position themselves a little higher than average (so a passing tip here is to become one of the world's richest people if you want to be slightly happier), but not much higher (because then you would already have heard about it).

One of the explanations for why they weren't happier about having surmounted all obstacles and limitations and collected all this money was that they had lost something of themselves somewhere along the path. Compared to people with average incomes, the rich believe that money is much more important for happiness, but they also have a much greater need to find themselves.

In short:

You can't spell happiness without the _I_.

I was so happy when I came across this clever saying. It rather neatly expresses how happiness is related to being yourself, in several ways.

To start with, your self-esteem affects your happiness. By recognizing your own self-worth, you can better enjoy being with other people, which is so critical to happiness. Your self-esteem also makes you less inclined to compare yourself to others and makes you more secure, so others will be more inclined to want to spend time with you (instead of, say, wanting to get at your money, if you're rich). Studies show that people with higher self-esteem find it easier to make new friends and are less stressed about work, housing, and other aspects of life. They also find it easier to be grateful for the good things in their lives (instead of worrying about being undeserving).

Now, the next thing I'm going to tell you will sound familiar. If you want to have higher self-esteem, you should choose your parents carefully. Because they affect not only your genetic qualities but have also been shown to play a large part in the development of their children's self-esteem. You can also act as your own parent and remind yourself that you are good and that you're good enough just the way you are. Researchers have carried out experiments with affirmations, in which people are asked to give themselves these kinds of reminders every day, and they found that their self-esteem had increased after only 2 weeks, making them a bit happier at the same time. So...

Remind yourself that you're good enough, just the way you are.

Another way of increasing your happiness is to develop your self-confidence. By feeling that you are good at something, you'll be in the flow state more, as I'm sure you remember. You'll *dare* to have the confidence that you're going to be able to deal with challenges, which means that you can celebrate early victories and get more from your happy moments in life. That makes it easier to believe that you can make a difference both for yourself and others, which in turn makes it easier to have faith and be kind.

The keyword in developing your self-confidence is *dare*. Dare to try things. Whether it's going down a ski slope, solving equations, getting your own initiatives through at work, or contacting somebody you're interested in. You don't need to take huge steps; you can start with the bunny slope or send a message on Facebook instead of walking up to somebody.

For every little step you take, you'll discover that you actually pulled it off (most of the time) or that it didn't actually hurt you to fail (sometimes), which means that you can dare to take another step and eventually you're cruising down a black diamond, or find yourself on a date with that person you've been admiring from a distance. So...

Dare to try.

A third way of increasing your happiness is to complement your self-confidence with self-*kindness*. In the same way that it's important to feel that you're good, it is also okay to not always be good. You aren't going to successfully deal with every challenge in life (I hope that wasn't a spoiler!), and if you are going to worry about that and feel ashamed and unsuccessful, then you might just as well start chain-smoking right now because you are not going to have a particularly long or happy life. If you don't believe me, you can check the references at the end of the book—they include a bunch of studies that show exactly that.

But there are also plenty of studies that show that self-kindness means that you don't need to be less happy when things don't go your way or when you don't live up to all those expectations that none of us can stop from setting for ourselves. Self-kindness also makes it easier to indulge yourself sometimes, which increases your happiness. You can allow yourself to enjoy life without basing that enjoyment on having achieved something or asking yourself whether you really deserve it. So...

Be kind to yourself.

A fourth way of increasing your happiness is to find yourself. That might sound a bit touchy-feely and make you think of backpacking in Australia (if you have the chance, though, you might want to indulge in that) or breaking up with somebody, but it's really about having an "independent definition of who you are," as a researcher would put it. Which means defining yourself by more than just your context (your job or your money) and other people's expectations of you. Otherwise life soon fills up with things that you're doing for other people, not because you yourself really want to do them.

When I carried out a study of 1,000 or so Swedes and asked them to write down what they had done during the day, I could see that the simplest way to separate those who were a little happier from those a little less happy was to count up how many things they did because they wanted to do them, minus the things they did because they felt that they had to. If you do lots of things because your partner makes you feel that you have to, instead of because you want to, then it isn't a cliché to say that you need to find yourself.

Finding yourself can also be about being the person you actually are and really want to be, instead of playing a role. Because you can't feel a sense of community if you aren't really taking part in it, and only wearing a title or label that you think others want you to have. You can't be present and celebrate life if you aren't actually there. So, throw in a bit of self-confidence and a bit of self-kindness and dare yourself to:

Discover yourself.

The last tip to increase your happiness is to be an extrovert—which is easy as pie if you already are an extrovert, and difficult as hell if you're an introvert. But there are so many studies precisely about how personality affects people's happiness that it feels more or less obligatory to mention this. The fact is, all of these studies point out the same thing: the worst thing for happiness is to be neurotic (surprise!) and the best is to be outgoing. Outgoing people show up over and over a little bit higher on the happiness scale. The reason being that they find it easier to seek contact with other people and are generally open to getting together with people, activities, and possibilities that make them happy.

I have personally always been shy and introverted and I know how hard it is to try to be an extrovert. But it has helped me to think about why extroverts are a bit happier and find my own ways of getting there. For example, by becoming friends with people on social media that I would otherwise never have met or dared to say hello to in real life. Or by writing columns or even books about the stuff I think about but find difficult to express in conversations, and inviting people into my life in that way (welcome, and thanks for reading; this makes me a little happier).

I can also recommend setting up a coffee date. There is, in fact, research showing that the body temperature of people who drink coffee raises a little, and that warmth means that they literally feel a bit more relaxed with other people (in experiments, people who have drunk coffee sit a bit closer to each other and talk a bit more). My guess is that it works with tea, too. Or meeting people at the gym. I love that: it increases your body temperature and gives you something in common to do and talk about (and besides you're so out of breath that you don't need to talk that much!).

»THE BODY TEMPERATURE OF PEOPLE WHO DRINK COFFEE RAISES A LITTLE AND THAT WARMTH MEANS THAT THEY LITERALLY FEEL A BIT MORE RELAXED WITH OTHER PEOPLE.«

13

DON'T TAKE HAPPINESS TOO SERIOUSLY

I WAS a visiting professor in Helsinki when Finland was first rated the happiest country in the world in the United Nations' *World Happiness Report* (a top spot they would hang on to for several years). I was naturally curious what it was that made them so happy. So, I asked just over 1,000 Finns to keep daily diaries and estimate how happy they were with everything from their career to their health, relationship, and leisure. Every week when they sent in their diaries I sat down eagerly and went through them, searching for patterns. My expectations of solving the riddle of Finnish happiness were great.

But no matter how I twisted and turned the numbers around, I couldn't find any clear patterns that would explain what made the Finns unique. Instead, after a few weeks, I discovered a totally different pattern: their responses decreased slowly but surely in every category.

The more they started to think about how happy they really were with the various parts of their lives as, time after time, they rated their happiness levels in their diaries—the less happy they felt.

I didn't feel like a particularly successful happiness researcher. In fact, I felt guilty when I realized that my measurements had just made the happiest people in the world not nearly as happy (sorry!).

So here is my last—and most important—tip to you:

Don't use that happiness scale at the beginning of the book too often.

Happiness is a really tough criterion to measure your life by. If your standard for, say, treating yourself to a chocolate truffle is, *Will I make myself happier by eating it?*, you probably won't indulge very often. This can, of course, be a good tip if you think you ought to eat fewer chocolate truffles. (You might even find it worth testing this on something you want to stop doing: perhaps you can eliminate the bad habit of biting your nails if every time you first stop and circle a number on the scale of happiness and ask, *Will this really make me happy?*). But you won't get many new friends, won't do what you are so good at, or stay together with your partner very much longer. (How many mornings do you actually sit at the breakfast table and think, *Oh, that person who eats their porridge with a smacking sound and whistles through their nose when they drink coffee makes me so happy?*)

All of that does make you happier: indulging yourself, being with friends, getting into the flow state and making a family. But if the goal every time you indulge is to be happy, then it will be extremely hard to choose. There are a lot of different chocolate truffles. Or perhaps you should choose a piece of cheesecake instead, or some candy. There are an awful lot of people you could become friends with. You can swipe until you dislocate your thumb before you've gone through all the potential partners in town.

If your goal with these things is to make yourself happy, then you're going to be fully occupied making your way between all the choices and you won't have time to do anything at all. Or else you'll just give up in despair. It's a bit like retirement saving plans: an American study showed that the sharp rise in retirement saving plan alternatives in the last few years has actually led to people putting aside *less* money instead of more.

Having happiness as a criterion also makes it a little more difficult to enjoy what you're doing. Researchers asked people if they think that you get happier by listening to music (which most people think you can, and which studies confirm—when you're listening to music you like). The subjects then listened to a happy song, and when subsequently asked about how much they enjoyed the music, on average they answered lower than other people, because having had the happiness question automatically made them think about happiness as a criterion when they listened. Some other researchers did a similar experiment with people who watched a film with the same result: those who thought about how movie-watching can make them happy didn't like watching the movies as much.

Happiness is a tough criterion to judge things by. It doesn't matter how exciting or funny a film is, if you are expecting it to be one of the highlights of your life, you can hardly be anything but disappointed. It's the same with life in general: if happiness is your permanent standard, it's as if your existence transforms into a long sequence of opportunities to achieve the highest result.

In recent times, some studies have been carried out which do indeed show that people who take happiness more seriously than others turn out to be a bit less happy than the average person. A bunch of researchers even tested the hypothesis that the hunt for happiness is linked to bipolar disorder (swinging between exaggerated hopes and disappointments) and depression and found that there actually was some connection. Not that we should be sounding a general alarm and declaring a national health warning—the effects aren't particularly significant, but, strange though they may sound, they exist nevertheless.

Happiness is too important to be taken seriously.

It affects how we feel, how long we live, what we do, and with whom we live. It turns us into better versions of ourselves, if we let it (by not getting in its way, or pushing it away being overly demanding).

Even the briefest moments and the very tiniest increases in the level of your happiness are fantastic and make *you* a little more fantastic. It can be about the math problem you just did, that short walk you took, the smile you share with somebody on the bus, the weekend you're looking forward to, or the chocolate bar you munch on a Tuesday morning.

And it doesn't make any difference if there's an even better chocolate bar to indulge in, a more challenging differential equation to solve, or an even lovelier partner to listen to when they slurp their morning coffee—in other words, an even greater happiness. Your happiness won't be worth less because of that.

Happiness is not an accomplishment which is better or worse; it is always good.

Nor is it a project or a plan.

It's that delightful feeling that can suddenly take you by surprise when you do one of the things we have taken up in earlier chapters. It comes and goes, and sometimes lasts a brief time, sometimes a bit longer. Sometimes it's big and sometimes a little smaller. But you can enjoy it just as much regardless.

You will never be done with it. Which is lovely, isn't it?

You don't even have to make a major effort, which I hope this book shows.

Does all of this apply to cleaner fish? you might be wondering. You know, those little fish that attach themselves to big fish or that exfoliate your feet when you stick them into a fishbowl at certain spas? It's funny you should ask that, because there's actually a study comparing the behaviors of humans and cleaner fish (and lots of other animals, but that will have to be the subject of another book). And the answer is no, it isn't the same for cleaner fish.

Be happy that you're not a cleaner fish.

PS: Does the book really end like that: "Be happy that you aren't a cleaner fish"? Yes, how else do you end a book about happiness? It's a subject that doesn't really have an endpoint. There's so much to say; I have chosen only a fraction of it, and we're learning more all the time. So this will have to do for the time being. Until another little book about happiness comes along? I look forward to writing that. And hereby indulge myself in ending this book with that reminder: Be happy that you you're not a cleaner fish.

»HAPPINESS IS A TOUGH CRITERION TO USE TO JUDGE THINGS. IT DOESN'T MATTER HOW EXCITING OR FUNNY A FILM IS, IF YOU ARE EXPECTING IT TO BE ONE OF THE HIGHLIGHTS OF YOUR LIFE THEN YOU CAN HARDLY BE ANYTHING BUT DISAPPOINTED.«

SOURCES

WHAT CAN HAPPINESS RESEARCH TEACH US?

Barak, Y. (2006). The immune system and happiness. *Autoimmunity reviews, 5*(8), 523–527.

Cummins, R. A. (2000). Personal income and subjective well-being: A review. *Journal of Happiness Studies, 1*, 133–158.

Dahlen, M. (2008). *Nextopia: livet, lyckan och pengarna i förväntningssamhället.* Stockholm: Volante.

Diener, E. & Diener, C. (1996). Most people are happy. *Psychological Science, 7*, 181–185.

Freud, S. (1929). *Das Unbehagen in der Kultur.* Wien: Internationaler Psychoanalytischer Verlag.

Helliwell, J. F. (2003). How's life? Combining individual and national variables to explain subjective well-being. *Economic Modelling, 20*, 331–360.

Lykken, D. T. & Tellegen, A. (1996). Happiness is a stochastic phenomenon. *Psychological Science, 7*, 186–189.

Lyubomirsky, S., King, L. A. & Diener, E. (2005). The benefits of frequent positive affect: Does happiness lead to success? *Psychological Bulletin, 131*, 803–855.

Myerson, A. (1917). Eupathics – A program for mental hygiene. *The Journal of Abnormal Psychology, 12*(5), 343.

1: CHOOSE YOUR PARENTS CAREFULLY (YES, IT CAN BE DONE)

Bartels, M. (2015). Genetics of wellbeing and its components satisfaction with life, happiness, and quality of life: A review and meta-analysis of heritability studies. *Behavior Genetics, 45*(2), 137–156.

Blum, K., et al. (2012). Neuropsychiatric genetics of happiness, friendships, and politics: hypothesizing homophily ("birds of a feather flock together") as a function of reward gene polymorphisms. *Journal of Genetic Syndrome & Gene Therapy*, 3(112).

Bouchard, T. J., Jr. & Loehlin, J. C. (2001). Genes, evolution, and personality. *Behavior Genetics*, 31, 243–273.

Crowley, J. J., et al. (2015). Analyses of allele-specific gene expression in highly divergent mouse crosses identifies pervasive allelic imbalance. *Nature Genetics*, 47(4), 353.

De Neve, J. E., Christakis, N. A., Fowler, J. H., & Frey, B. S. (2012). Genes, economics, and happiness. *Journal of Neuroscience, Psychology, and Economics*, 5(4), 193.

DeNeve, K. M., & Cooper, H. (1998). The happy personality: A meta-analysis of 137 personality traits and subjective well-being. *Psychological Bulletin*, 124, 197–229.

Halabe Bucay et al. (2009). Endorphins, personality, and inheritance: Establishing the biochemical bases of inheritance. *Bioscience Hypotheses*, 2(3), 170–171.

Headey, B., Muffels, R. & Wagner, G. G. (2014). Parents transmit happiness along with associated values and behaviors to their children: A lifelong happiness dividend? *Social Indicators Research*, 116(3), 909–933.

Lykken, D. T., Bouchard, T. J., Jr., McGue, M. & Tellegen, A. (1990). The Minnesota Twin Family Registry: Some initial findings. *Acta Geneticae Medicae et Gemellologiae*, 39, 35–70.

Minkov, M. & Bond, M. H. (2017). A genetic component to national differences in happiness. *Journal of Happiness Studies*, 18(2), 321–340.

Nes, R. B. (2010). Happiness in behaviour genetics: Findings and implications. *Journal of Happiness Studies*, 11(3), 369–381.

Nes, R. B. & Røysamb, E. (2017). Happiness in behaviour genetics: An update on heritability and changeability. *Journal of Happiness Studies*, 18(5), 1533–1552.

Nes, R. B., et al. (2006). Subjective well-being: Genetic and environmental contributions to stability and change. *Psychological Medicine*, 36, 1033–1042.

Oishi, S., Graham, J., Kesebir, S. & Galinha, I. C. (2013). Concepts of happiness across time and cultures. *Personality and Social Psychology Bulletin*, 39(5), 559–577.

Rietveld, C. A., et al. (2013). Molecular genetics and subjective well-being. *Proceedings of the National Academy of Sciences*, 110(24), 9692–9697.

Weiss, A., Bates, T. C. & Luciano, M. (2008). Happiness is a personal(ity) thing: The genetics of personality and well-being in a representative sample. *Psychological Science*, 19, 3, 205–210.

Weiss, A., King, J. E., & Enns, R. M. (2002). Subjective well-being is heritable and genetically correlated with dominance in chimpanzees (Pan troglodytes). *Journal of Personality and Social Psychology*, 83, 1141–1149.

2: BELIEVE

Aghababaei, N., et al. (2016). Predicting subjective well-being by religious and scientific attitudes with hope, purpose in life, and death anxiety as mediators. *Personality and Individual Differences*, 90, 93–98.

Blazer, D. & Palmore, E. (1976). Religion and aging in a longitudinal panel. *The Gerontologist*, 16(1), 82–85.

Beezhold, B. L. & Johnston, C. S. (2012). Restriction of meat, fish, and poultry in omnivores improves mood: A pilot randomized controlled trial. *Nutrition Journal*, 11(9). doi:10.1186/1475-2891-11-9

Campante, F. & Yanagizawa-Drott, D. (2015). Does religion affect economic growth and happiness? Evidence from Ramadan. *The Quarterly Journal of Economics*, 130(2), 615–658.

Fenelon, A. & Danielsen, S. (2016). Leaving my religion: Understanding the relationship between religious disaffiliation, health, and well-being. *Social Science Research*, 57, 49–62.

Ferriss, A. L. (2002). Religion and the quality of life. *Journal of Happiness Studies*, 3(3), 199–215.

Headey, B., Schupp, J., Tucci, I. & Wagner, G. G. (2010). Authentic happiness theory supported by impact of religion on life satisfaction: A longitudinal analysis with data for Germany. *The Journal of Positive Psychology*, 5(1), 73–82.

How vegetarians are almost twice as likely to be suffering from depression as those who love meat. *Daily Mail.* (2017, 5 August). Retrieved 2019-11-18 from https://www.dailymail.co.uk/health/article-4762624/Vegetarians-likely-glum-meat-eaters.html

Kosher, H. & Ben-Arieh, A. (2017). Religion and subjective well-being among children: A comparison of six religion groups. *Children and Youth Services Review*, 80, 63–77.

Kwon, J. Y., Bercovici, H. L., Cunningham, K. & Varnum, M. E. (2018). How will we react to the discovery of extraterrestrial life? *Frontiers in Psychology*, 8, 2308.

Lelkes, O. (2006). Tasting freedom: Happiness, religion and economic transition. *Journal of Economic Behavior & Organization*, 59(2), 173–194.

Lifshin, U., Greenberg, J., Weise, D. & Soenke, M. (2016). It's the end of the world and I feel fine: Soul belief and perceptions of end-of-the-world scenarios. *Personality and Social Psychology Bulletin*, 42(1), 104–117.

Petrovic, P., et al. (2005). Placebo in emotional processing—induced expectations of anxiety relief activate a generalized modulatory network. *Neuron*, 46(6), 957–969.

Swinyard, W. R., Kau, A. K. & Phua, H. Y. (2001). Happiness, materialism, and religious experience in the US and Singapore. *Journal of Happiness Studies*, 2(1), 13–32.

3: CLAIM VICTORY IN ADVANCE

Bjärehed, J., Sarkohi, A. & Andersson, G. (2010). Less positive or more negative? Future-directed thinking in mild to moderate depression. *Cognitive Behaviour Therapy*, 39(1), 37–45.

Li, J., Wang, X. & Hovy, E. (2014 November). What a nasty day: Exploring mood-weather relationship from twitter. In *Proceedings of the 23rd ACM International Conference on Conference on Information and Knowledge Management* (pp. 1309–1318). New York: ACM.

Littman-Ovadia, H. & Nir, D. (2014). Looking forward to tomorrow: The buffering effect of a daily optimism intervention. *The Journal of Positive Psychology*, 9(2), 122–136.

MacLeod, A. K. & Conway, C. (2005). Well-being and the anticipation of future positive experiences: The role of income, social networks, and planning ability. *Cognition & Emotion*, 19(3), 357–374.

MacLeod, A. K. & Conway, C. (2007). Well-being and positive future thinking for the self versus others. *Cognition and Emotion*, 21(5), 1114–1124.

MacLeod, A. K., Coates, E. & Hetherton, J. (2008). Increasing well-being through teaching goal-setting and planning skills: Results of a brief intervention. *Journal of Happiness Studies*, 9(2), 185–196.

Peters, M. L., Flink, I. K., Boersma, K. & Linton, S. J. (2010). Manipulating optimism: Can imagining a best possible self be used to increase positive future expectancies? *The Journal of Positive Psychology*, 5(3), 204–211.

Quoidbach, J., Wood, A. M. & Hansenne, M. (2009). Back to the future: The effect of daily practice of mental time travel into the future on happiness and anxiety. *The Journal of Positive Psychology*, 4(5), 349–355.

Robinson, M. D. & Ryff, C. D. (1999). The role of self-deception in perceptions of past, present, and future happiness. *Personality and Social Psychology Bulletin*, 25(5), 596–608.

Stuber, G. D., Wightman, R. M. & Carelli, R. M. (2005). Extinction of cocaine self-administration reveals functionally and temporally distinct dopaminergic signals in the nucleus accumbens. *Neuron*, 46(4), 661–669.

4: CELEBRATE

Borelli, J. L., Rasmussen, H. F., Burkhart, M. L. & Sbarra, D. A. (2015). Relational savoring in long-distance romantic relationships. *Journal of Social and Personal Relationships*, 32(8), 1083–1108.

Dahlen, M. (2016). *Kaosologi*. Stockholm: Volante.

Goodman, J. K., Malkoc, S. A. & Stephenson, B. L. (2016). Celebrate or commemorate? A material purchase advantage when honoring special life events. *Journal of the Association for Consumer Research*, 1(4), 497–508.

Jose, P. E., Lim, B. T. & Bryant, F. B. (2012). Does savoring increase happiness? A daily diary study. *The Journal of Positive Psychology*, 7(3), 176–187.

Kurtz, J. L. (2008). Looking to the future to appreciate the present: The benefits of perceived temporal scarcity. *Psychological Science*, 19(12), 1238–1241.

Loewenstein, G., Krishnamurti, T., Kopsic, J. & McDonald, D. (2015). Does increased sexual frequency enhance happiness? *Journal of Economic Behavior & Organization*, 116, 206–218.

Muise, A., Schimmack, U. & Impett, E. A. (2016). Sexual frequency predicts greater well-being, but more is not always better. *Social Psychological and Personality Science*, 7(4), 295–302.

Quoidbach, J., Berry, E. V., Hansenne, M. & Mikolajczak, M. (2010). Positive emotion regulation and well-being: Comparing the impact of eight savoring and dampening strategies. *Personality and Individual Differences*, 49(5), 368–373.

Ramsey, M. A. & Gentzler, A. L. (2014). Age differences in subjective well-being across adulthood: The roles of savoring and future time perspective. *The International Journal of Aging and Human Development*, 78(1), 3–22.

5: RELIVE

Aaker, J. L., Rudd, M. & Mogilner, C. (2011). If money does not make you happy, consider time. *Journal of consumer psychology*, 21(2), 126–130.

Bryant, F. B., Smart, C. M. & King, S. P. (2005). Using the past to enhance the present: Boosting happiness through positive reminiscence. *Journal of Happiness Studies*, 6(3), 227–260.

Cheung, W. Y., et al. (2013). Back to the future: Nostalgia increases optimism. *Personality and Social Psychology Bulletin*, 39(11), 1484–1496.

Hirsch, A. R. (1992). Nostalgia: a neuropsychiatric understanding. In J. F. Sherry, Jr. & B. Sterrnthal (Eds.), *North American Advances in Consumer Research* (vol. 19, pp. 390–395). Provo, UT: Association for Consumer Research.

Mogilner, C., Kamvar, S. D. & Aaker, J. (2011). The shifting meaning of happiness. *Social Psychological and Personality Science*, 2(4), 395–402.

Routledge, C., Wildschut, T., Sedikides, C. & Juhl, J. (2013). Nostalgia as a resource for psychological health and well-being. *Social and Personality Psychology Compass*, 7(11), 808–818.

Sedikides, C., Wildschut, T., Arndt, J. & Routledge, C. (2008). Nostalgia: Past, present, and future. *Current Directions in Psychological Science*, 17(5), 304–307.

6: INDULGE YOURSELF

Blanchflower, D. G. & Oswald, A. J. (2004). Money, sex and happiness: An empirical study. *Scandinavian Journal of Economics*, 106(3), 393–415.

Dahlen, M. (2019). *Starkt kul*. Stockholm: Volante.

Gruber, J., Mauss, I. B. & Tamir, M. (2011). A dark side of happiness? How, when, and why happiness is not always good. *Perspectives on Psychological Science*, 6(3), 222–233.

Koch, A. B. (2018). Children's Perspectives on Happiness and Subjective Well-being in Preschool. *Children & Society*, 32(1), 73–83.

Schooler, J. W., Ariely, D. & Loewenstein, G. (2003). The pursuit and assessment of happiness may be self-defeating. In J. C. I. Brocas (Ed.), *The psychology of economic decisions: Rationality and well-being* (pp. 41–70). Oxford: Oxford University Press.

Why being naughty helps you feel younger. *The Telegraph.* (2009, 22 July). Retrieved 2019-11-18 from https://www.telegraph.co.uk/news/uknews/5882245/Why-being-naughty-helps- you-feel-younger.html

Xu, J. & Schwarz, N. (2009). Do we really need a reason to indulge? *Journal of Marketing Research*, 46(1), 25–36.

Ziv, I., Lubin, O. B. H. & Asher, S. (2018). "I swear I will never betray you": Factors reported by spouses as helping them resist extramarital sex in relation to gender, marriage length, and religiosity. *The Journal of Sex Research*, 55(2), 236–251.

7: GET SOME EXERCISE

Costa, T., Galati, D. & Rognoni, E. (2009). The Hurst exponent of cardiac response to positive and negative emotional film stimuli using wavelet. *Autonomic Neuroscience*, 151(2), 183–185.

Courneya, K. S., et al. (2009). Randomized controlled trial of the effects of aerobic exercise on physical functioning and quality of life in lymphoma patients. *Journal of Clinical Oncology*, 27(27), 4605–4612.

Huang, H. & Humphreys, B. R. (2012). Sports participation and happiness: Evidence from US microdata. *Journal of Economic Psychology*, 33(4), 776–793.

Khazaee-Pool, M., Sadeghi, R., Majlessi, F. & Rahimi Foroushani, A. (2015). Effects of physical exercise programme on happiness among older people. *Journal of Psychiatric and Mental Health Nursing*, 22(1), 47–57.

Kye, S. Y. & Park, K. (2014). Health-related determinants of happiness in Korean adults. *International Journal of Public Health*, 59(5), 731–738.

Lathia, N., Sandstrom, G. M., Mascolo, C. & Rentfrow, P. J. (2017). Happier people live more active lives: Using smartphones to link happiness and physical activity. *PLoS ONE* 12(1): e0160589.

Leuenberger, A. (2006). Endorphins, exercise, and addictions: a review of exercise dependence. *The Premier Journal for Undergraduate Publications in the Neurosciences*, 3, 1–9.

Olsson, L. E., et al. (2013). Happiness and satisfaction with work commute. *Social Indicators Research*, 111(1), 255–263.

Rasmussen, M. & Laumann, K. (2014). The role of exercise during adolescence on adult happiness and mood. *Leisure Studies*, 33(4), 341–356.

Richards, J., et al. (2015). Don't worry, be happy: cross-sectional associations between physical activity and happiness in 15 European countries. *BMC Public Health*, 15(1), 53.

Rimm-Kaufman, S. E. & Kagan, J. (1996). The psychological significance of changes in skin temperature. *Motivation and Emotion*, 20(1), 63–78.

Salesi, M. & Jowkar, B. (2011). Effects of exercise and physical activity on happiness of postmenopausal female. *Iranian Journal of Ageing*, 6(2).

Wang, F., et al. (2012). Long-term association between leisure-time physical activity and changes in happiness: analysis of the Prospective National Population Health Survey. *American Journal of Epidemiology*, 176(12), 1095–1100.

8: GET IN THE FLOW

Carr, A. (2013). *Positive psychology: The science of happiness and human strengths*. Routledge.

Clarke, S. G. & Haworth, J. T. (1994). "Flow" experience in the daily lives of sixth-form college students. *British Journal of Psychology*, 85(4), 511–523.

Collins, A. L., Sarkisian, N. & Winner, E. (2009). Flow and happiness in later life: An investigation into the role of daily and weekly flow experiences. *Journal of Happiness Studies*, 10(6), 703–719.

Csíkszentmihályi, M. (1997). Happiness and creativity. *The Futurist*, 31(5), S8.

Csíkszentmihályi, M. & Hunter, J. (2003). Happiness in everyday life: The uses of experience sampling. *Journal of Happiness Studies*, 4(2), 185–199.

Csíkszentmihályi, M. & Wong, M. M. H. (2014). The situational and personal correlates of happiness: A cross-national comparison. In *Flow and the foundations of positive psychology* (pp. 69–88). Dordrecht: Springer.

Fisher, C. D. (2010). Happiness at work. *International Journal of Management Reviews*, 12(4), 384–412.

Hull, D. C., Williams, G. A. & Griffiths, M. D. (2013). Video game characteristics, happiness and flow as predictors of addiction among video game players: A pilot study. *Journal of Behavioral Addictions*, 2(3), 145–152.

Tsaur, S. H., Yen, C. H. & Hsiao, S. L. (2013). Transcendent experience, flow and happiness for mountain climbers. *International Journal of Tourism Research*, 15(4), 360–374.

9: BE NiCE

Aknin, L. B., Broesch, T., Hamlin, J. K. & Van de Vondervoort, J. W. (2015). Prosocial behavior leads to happiness in a small-scale rural society. *Journal of Experimental Psychology: General*, 144(4), 788.

Aknin, L. B., Hamlin, J. K. & Dunn, E. W. (2012). Giving leads to happiness in young children. *PLoS ONE*, 7(6), e39211.

Aknin, L. B., Dunn, E. W. & Norton, M. I. (2012). Happiness runs in a circular motion: Evidence for a positive feedback loop between pro-social spending and happiness. *Journal of Happiness Studies*, 13(2), 347–355.

Drayton, L. A., & Santos, L. R. (2016). Is Human Prosocial Behavior Unique? *Positive Neuroscience*, 73.

Dunn, E. W., Aknin, L. B. & Norton, M. I. (2008). Spending money on others promotes happiness. *Science*, 319(5870), 1687–1688.

Harbaugh, W. T., Mayr, U. & Burghart, D. R. (2007). Neural responses to taxation and voluntary giving reveal motives for charitable donations. *Science*, 316(5831), 1622–1625.

Kerr, S. L., O'Donovan, A. & Pepping, C. A. (2015). Can gratitude and kindness interventions enhance well-being in a clinical sample? *Journal of Happiness Studies*, 16(1), 17–36.

Layous, K., et al. (2012). Kindness counts: Prompting prosocial behavior in preadolescents boosts peer acceptance and well-being. *PLoS ONE*, 7(12), e51380.

Otake, K., et al. (2006). Happy people become happier through kindness: A counting kindnesses intervention. *Journal of Happiness Studies*, 7(3), 361–375.

Post, S. G. (2005). Altruism, happiness, and health: It's good to be good. *International Journal of Behavioral Medicine*, 12(2), 66–77.

Wu, K., Chen, C. & Greenberger, E. (2019). Nice guys and gals can finish first: Personality and speed-dating success among Asian Americans. *Journal of Social and Personal Relationships*, 36(8), 2507–2527.

10: BE GRATEFUL

Abou-Zeid, M. & Ben-Akiva, M. (2011). The effect of social comparisons on commute well-being. *Transportation Research Part A: Policy and Practice*, 45(4), 345–361.

Algoe, S. B. & Haidt, J. (2009). Witnessing excellence in action: The "other-praising" emotions of elevation, gratitude, and admiration. *The Journal of Positive Psychology*, 4(2), 105–127.

Ball, R. & Chernova, K. (2008). Absolute income, relative income, and happiness. *Social Indicators Research*, 88(3), 497–529.

Dahlen, M. (2008). *Nextopia*. Stockholm: Volante.

Dahlen, M. (2016). *Kaosologi*. Stockholm: Volante.

Kohler, H. P., Behrman, J. R. & Skytthe, A. (2005). Partner + children = happiness? The effects of partnerships and fertility on well-being. *Population and Development Review*, 31(3), 407–445.

McCraty, R., et al. (1995). The effects of emotions on short-term power spectrum analysis of heart rate variability. *The American Journal of Cardiology*, 76(14), 1089–1093.

McCullough, M. E. & Emmons, R. A. (2003). Counting blessings versus burdens: An experimental investigation of gratitude and subjective well-being in daily life. *Journal of Personality and Social Psychology*, 84(2), 377–389.

McCullough, M. E., Tsang, J. A. & Emmons, R. A. (2004). Gratitude in intermediate affective terrain: links of grateful moods to individual differences and daily emotional experience. *Journal of Personality and Social Psychology*, 86(2), 295.

Seligman, Martin E. P. (2012). *Flourish: A visionary new understanding of happiness and well-being*. New York: Simon and Schuster.

Wadsworth, T. (2014). Sex and the pursuit of happiness: How other people's sex lives are related to our sense of well-being. *Social Indicators Research*, 116(1), 115–135.

11: *BE TOGETHER*

Binetti, N., et al. (2016). Pupil dilation as an index of preferred mutual gaze duration. *Royal Society Open Science*, 3(7), 160086.

Bliss, C. A., et al. (2012). Twitter reciprocal reply networks exhibit assortativity with respect to happiness. *Journal of Computational Science*, 3(5), 388–397.

Capaldi, C. A., Dopko, R. L. & Zelenski, J. M. (2014). The relationship between nature connectedness and happiness: a meta-analysis. *Frontiers in Psychology*, 5, 976.

Daniel Jr, E. S. & Westerman, D. K. (2017). Valar Morghulis (all parasocial men must die): having nonfictional responses to a fictional character. *Communication Research Reports*, 34(2), 143–152.

Donnar, G. (2017). "Food porn" or intimate sociality: committed celebrity and cultural performances of overeating in meokbang. *Celebrity Studies*, 8(1), 122–127.

Fowler, J. H. & Christakis, N. A. (2008). Dynamic spread of happiness in a large social network: longitudinal analysis over 20 years in the Framingham Heart Study. *BMJ*, 337, a2338.

Gray, H. M., Ishii, K. & Ambady, N. (2011). Misery loves company: When sadness increases the desire for social connectedness. *Personality and Social Psychology Bulletin*, 37(11), 1438–1448.

Helliwell, J. F. & Huang, H. (2013). Comparing the happiness effects of real and on-line friends. *PLoS ONE*, 8(9), e72754.

Hendrickson, B., Rosen, D. & Aune, R. K. (2011). An analysis of friendship networks, social connectedness, homesickness, and satisfaction levels of international students. *International Journal of Intercultural Relations, 35*(3), 281–295.

Holder, M. D. & Coleman, B. (2009). The contribution of social relationships to children's happiness. *Journal of Happiness Studies,* 10(3), 329–349.

Kim, J. & Lee, J. E. R. (2011). The Facebook paths to happiness: Effects of the number of Facebook friends and self-presentation on subjective well-being. *Cyberpsychology, Behavior, and Social Networking,* 14(6), 359–364.

Leyden, K. M., Goldberg, A. & Michelbach, P. (2011). Understanding the pursuit of happiness in ten major cities. *Urban Affairs Review,* 47(6), 861–888.

Lin, R. & Utz, S. (2015). The emotional responses of browsing Facebook: Happiness, envy, and the role of tie strength. *Computers in human behavior, 52,* 29–38.

Mauss, I. B., et al. (2011). Don't hide your happiness! Positive emotion dissociation, social connectedness, and psychological functioning. *Journal of Personality and Social Psychology,* 100(4), 738.

Sandstrom, G. M. & Dunn, E. W. (2014). Is efficiency overrated? Minimal social interactions lead to belonging and positive affect. *Social Psychological and Personality Science, 5*(4), 437–442.

Satici, S. A., Uysal, R. & Deniz, M. E. (2016). Linking social connectedness to loneliness: The mediating role of subjective happiness. *Personality and Individual Differences, 97,* 306–310.

Striano, T., Kopp, F., Grossmann, T. & Reid, V. M. (2006). Eye contact influences neural processing of emotional expressions in 4-month-old infants. *Social Cognitive and Affective Neuroscience,* 1(2), 87–94.

12: BE YOURSELF

Caprara, G. V., et al. (2006). Looking for adolescents' well-being: Self-efficacy beliefs as determinants of positive thinking and happiness. *Epidemiology and Psychiatric Sciences,* 15(1), 30–43.

Cheng, H. & Furnham, A. (2003). Personality, self-esteem, and demographic predictions of happiness and depression. *Personality and Individual Differences*, 34(6), 921–942.

Dahlen, M. (2016). *Kaosologi*. Stockholm: Volante.

Diener, E., Horwitz, J. & Emmons, R. A. (1985). Happiness of the very wealthy. *Social Indicators Research*, 16(3), 263–274.

Elliott, I. & Coker, S. (2008). Independent self-construal, self-reflection, and self-rumination: a path model for predicting happiness. *Australian Journal of Psychology*, 60(3), 127–134.

Furnham, A. & Cheng, H. (2000). Perceived parental behaviour, self-esteem and happiness. *Social Psychiatry and Psychiatric Epidemiology*, 35(10), 463–470.

Neff, K. D. (2011). Self-compassion, self-esteem, and well-being. *Social and personality psychology compass*, 5(1), 1–12.

Nelson, S. K., Fuller, J. A., Choi, I. & Lyubomirsky, S. (2014). Beyond self-protection: Self-affirmation benefits hedonic and eudaimonic well-being. *Personality and Social Psychology Bulletin*, 40(8), 998–1011.

Pavot, W., Diener, E. D. & Fujita, F. (1990). Extraversion and happiness. *Personality and Individual Differences*, 11(12), 1299–1306.

Tamir, M. (2009). Differential preferences for happiness: Extraversion and trait-consistent emotion regulation. *Journal of Personality*, 77(2), 447–470.

Williams, L. E. & Bargh, J. A. (2008). Experiencing physical warmth promotes interpersonal warmth. *Science*, 322(5901), 606–607.

Yuki, M., Sato, K., Takemura, K. & Oishi, S. (2013). Social ecology moderates the association between self-esteem and happiness. *Journal of Experimental Social Psychology*, 49(4), 741–746.

13: DON'T TAKE HAPPINESS TOO SERIOUSLY

Ford, B. Q., et al. (2015). Culture shapes whether the pursuit of happiness predicts higher or lower well-being. *Journal of Experimental Psychology: General*, 144(6), 1053.

Ford, B. Q., et al. (2014). Desperately seeking happiness: Valuing happiness is associated with symptoms and diagnosis of depression. *Journal of social and clinical psychology*, 33(10), 890–905.

Mauss, I. B., Tamir, M., Anderson, C. L. & Savino, N. S. (2011). Can seeking happiness make people unhappy? Paradoxical effects of valuing happiness. *Emotion*, 11(4), 807.

Schooler, J., Ariely, D. & Loewenstein, G. (2003). The pursuit and assessment of happiness may be self-defeating. In J. C. I. Brocas (Ed.), *The psychology of economic decisions: Rationality and well-being* (pp. 41–70). Oxford: Oxford University Press.